Catholic and American: The Political Theology of John Courtney Murray

Thomas P. Ferguson

Sheed & Ward

Sheed & Ward™ is a service of The National Catholic Reporter Publishing Company.

Library of Congress Cataloguing in Publication Data

Ferguson, Thomas P., 1966-
    Catholic and American : the political theology of John Courtney
Murray / Thomas P. Ferguson.
      p.   cm.
    Includes bibliographical references and index.
    ISBN: 1-55612-650-6 (alk. paper)
    1. Christianity and politics--History of doctrines--20th century.
2. Murray, John Courtney. 3. Freedom of religion--History--20th
century. 4. Catholic Church--Doctrines--History--20th century.
BX1793.F47 1993
261.7'092--dc20   93-1220
                                                  CIP

Published by: Sheed & Ward
                    115 E. Armour Blvd.
                    P.O. Box 419492
                    Kansas City, MO 64141

To order, call: (800) 333-7373

Cover design by John Murello.

Contents

Acknowledgements

THERE ARE MANY PEOPLE WHO HAVE BEEN A GREAT SOURCE OF encouragement to me since I first developed an interest in the contribution which John Courtney Murray made to our understanding of how we are continually called to seek creative solutions to the problem of incarnating the principles of Catholic social thought in ever-changing historical and political circumstances. I would like briefly to acknowledge those whose roles in the development of this project especially deserve public recognition.

"No pupil outranks his teacher," and so I first express my gratitude to several professors with whom I have had the privilege to study. At Allentown College of St. Francis de Sales, Bernard F. O'Connor, O.S.F.S. and Bernard F. Donahue, O.S.F.S. fanned into a flame the first sparks of my desire to pursue the study of political theory and guided me toward the University of Virginia where Michael Brint, Kenneth W. Thompson, and Dante L. Germino assisted me in my study of Murray's political theology as mentors, critics, and friends. I have also received a great deal of support in my efforts to bring this work to fruition from the faculty and staff of Mount Saint Mary's Seminary.

I am also grateful to members of the Society of Jesus who have encouraged me to pursue this study of the work of their confrere. I would especially like to thank Gerald P. Fogarty, S.J. who has generously assisted me first in serving as a reader of my doctoral dissertation, and then in helping me produce a manuscript suitable for publication. At the Woodstock Theological Center, Eugene Rooney, S.J. made valuable library resources available to me, and J. Leon Hooper, S.J. discussed my ideas and read my manuscript at various stages in their development.

To Robert Heyer, Editor-in-Chief at Sheed & Ward, who has enthusiastically sought to disseminate the wisdom of John Courtney

Murray through the publication of this work, I also express my heartfelt thanks.

The study I have undertaken was never intended to close the debate on any of the issues I have raised. If readers are inclined to respond critically to my thoughts with intelligence and civility, I will be satisfied that I have offered something valuable to the effort to assess the contribution of John Courtney Murray to the life of the Church and American society.

I dedicate all of my efforts, and any good that may come from them, to my family, whose love and support have animated this project from start to finish.

Thomas P. Ferguson

Introduction

AMERICAN CATHOLICS OFTEN FACE THE VEXATIOUS PROBLEM OF choosing between what seem to be equally desirable but ultimately incompatible goods. On the one hand, they are committed by faith to those religious principles which they hold to be absolute truths. On the other hand, they also feel a deep and abiding commitment to preserve and protect that Constitution which not only guarantees their freedom to hold and practice these religious beliefs but also guarantees others the right to dissent from these beliefs.

American Catholics also recognize that these traditions which they value so greatly are not simply contemporary phenomena. The Catholic Church, established as an historical institution by Jesus of Nazareth, is nearly 2000 years old. Likewise, the United States of America also enjoys a certain status as one of the world's most stable political regimes.

Given the historical consciousness of American Catholics, it is no wonder that the Catholic Church in America very frequently confronts the existential dilemma of applying what it holds to be universal principles in ever-changing historical circumstances. American Catholics, as Americans, and as Catholics, affirm that their political and religious beliefs are grounded in principles that are based on an objective reality. This community of civic-minded believers recognizes a very real continuity between its experience and that of its ancestors. Therefore, American Catholics believe that there must be some link to the past beyond a simple chronological progression of pragmatic advances or the individual innovations of a series of world-historical figures.

The political task facing American Catholics is very complex indeed. The application of universal principles in particular historical circumstances cannot be accomplished by means of a simple technical or mechanical manipulation of persons and resources by an elite corps of social scientists. The mediation between the universal and the contingent requires the exercise of the virtue of *prudence* (i.e., practical wisdom) on the part of those who would promote the establishment of a good society.

This mediation becomes the task of all American Catholics in some way or another. Catholic politicians in the American political process must integrate the demands placed on their consciences by the norms of moral behavior with the demands of the common good of all of the citizens of this country. Catholic men and women who participate in other forms of public service (e.g., health care, education, the arts, etc.) must also integrate the imperatives of their consciences with those of the common good. Likewise, all Catholic citizens who affirm the value of American participatory democracy must consider the best manner of promoting their vision of the good society as they cast their votes for their elected officials.

The task of mediating universal principles of faith in the historical reality of a religiously pluralistic society also falls to those philosophers and theologians who reflect on the social dimensions of this experience and are collectively known as "political theorists." These theorists (like their counterparts at all other levels of the political process) are eminently qualified to read the "signs of the times" as they experience the relativities and contingencies of the historical period in which they live. Unlike those citizens who are primarily pragmatically-oriented, however, these theorists also make a great effort to understand the underlying principles and values which provide the impetus for the actions of those who compete in the arena of practical politics.

John Courtney Murray, S.J. (1904-1967) was one of these theorists who consciously attempted to integrate the values of both Roman Catholicism and American democratic republicanism. Murray always remained a loyal citizen while simultaneously maintaining his commitment to the truth claims of his community of faith. He was a profound thinker whose greatest legacy was his *corpus* of writings in which he explained the tenuous compatibility between the ethical imperatives of Roman Catholic theology and American political philosophy.

In this work, I will attempt to explain and evaluate John Courtney Murray's solution to the problem of maintaining a commitment to the truths of Catholicism within the social reality of American religious pluralism. Murray steadfastly defended the notion that there is no necessary incompatibility between the Church established by Jesus Christ and the government established by the United States Constitution. His wisdom is of great value to both non-Catholic Americans and non-American Catholics. The purpose of this work, however, is primarily to consider Murray's teaching in light of the American Catholic experience.

Murray began his study of the American Catholic's relationship to Church and state by first describing in abstract terms the social nature of the human person. Every human person, he claimed, is a member of both a sacred and a secular society. By implication, therefore, the American Catholic is both a member of the universal Church and a citizen of the United States.

Murray then described the agents or institutions which may legitimately claim authority over the individual. He argued that the Church alone may legitimately exercise authority in the sacred or spiritual realm. In the secular or temporal society, however, the state[1] possesses only limited competence or power—it is only one of a number of authoritative orders which also include cultural, educational, economic, and religious institutions.

Murray insisted that the *abstract* distinction of the spiritual and temporal societies was necessary but not sufficient to resolve the dilemmas faced by American Catholics as they sought to establish a proper relationship between Church and state. Additionally, American Catholics must continually consider whether the abstract principles describing the proper relationship between religion and politics are manifest in the institutional relationship of Church and state as it exists in a particular *historical* situation.

In his effort to assess the compatibility of the Church's universal
and immutable truths and the practical principles of American democracy, Murray immediately encountered resistance from his contemporaries who proposed an alternative understanding of the Church's "official" teaching. These theologians taught that in the ideal temporal
social order (the *thesis*), the Catholic Church, by virtue of its authoritative role in the spiritual realm, ought also to be the established religion of the state. Where such an establishment was not possible (due
to the minority status of Catholics in a particular country), the only
acceptable condition (the *hypothesis*) would be the toleration of all
religious beliefs such that the Catholic Church possessed the same
freedom as all other religious groups.

As a Catholic, Murray was indeed committed to the truth of his
faith. As an American, however, he could not be convinced that the
arrangement of institutions and the guarantees of freedom found in
this country constituted a "second-best" or "*hypothesis*" situation. He
ardently believed that if democracy was not the best form of government, it was at least better than any other the world has known.

Murray's dissatisfaction with his contemporaries' articulation of
the truth of the Catholic faith prompted him to initiate an investigation
of the sources of Catholic teaching regarding the proper relationship
between religion and politics. After undertaking a truly strenuous
analysis of this problem, he discovered that if one looked beyond the
polemical writings of Robert Bellarmine and Leo XIII (whom his contemporaries cited almost exclusively as authoritative teachers), and returned to the political theory of Pope Gelasius I and John of Paris, one
might find the authentic principles of Catholic teaching *vis à vis* the
relationship between the sacred and the secular societies. Given a correct understanding of these universal principles, one might then conclude that the *thesis/hypothesis* distinction itself was simply a contingent formulation of Catholic teaching regarding the proper relationship
between Church and state. Having established these premises, Murray
argued that the Church in the twentieth century ought to reconsider its
understanding of religious liberty as it investigated the most appropriate manner of ordering the relationship between religion and politics.

In the course of his theological investigations, Murray did indeed
reclaim authentic principles of Catholic doctrine. However, his work

was also iconoclastic in the age in which he was writing. In fact, so strong was the resistance to Murray's theological and philosophical justification of the relationship of Church and state as it existed in the United States that his writings were subjected to censorship, and he ceased publishing articles on the subject of religious liberty between 1955 and 1963. His genius was recognized by the Fathers of the Second Vatican Council, however, when he was invited to attend that ecumenical council as a *peritus* (i.e., expert) in 1963. His extensive labors reached their ultimate fruition in 1965 when the Council approved the Declaration on Religious Liberty and thus gave a magisterial *imprimatur* to his contributions to Roman Catholic theology.[2]

Murray was not content with merely justifying the American constitutional system and its grant of freedom to all religious groups, however. He also proposed a philosophical method for political reasoning in a social environment such as that found in the United States. He believed that a social ethic rooted in the ancient and medieval natural law tradition represented the only possible basis for the establishment of a public consensus in a religiously pluralistic society. Additionally, he argued that such a natural law social ethic was entirely consistent with the philosophical bases of the American constitutional system.

Murray's analysis included a critique of his contemporaries' failure to recognize what he considered to be one of the first principles of the American Proposition—i.e., the multi-dimensional quality of human social existence which definitively circumscribes the authority of the state and thus frees the citizen to become fully human in both a spiritual and temporal sense. He claimed that as states transgressed the limits of their proper authority, peoples would begin to experience the obliteration of the distinction between the sacred and the secular. The consequences of these trends, he warned, were nothing less than the spiritual enslavement of the American people and the secularization of American society.

John Courtney Murray was indeed an intellectual giant of his age. His attempt to integrate Catholic social thought with the principles of the American Proposition marked a great advance in the ongoing endeavor to mediate the demands of universal principles in particular historical circumstances.

In an effort to remain faithful to the spirit which Murray himself brought to the project of theological inquiry, this work will proceed in a dialectical fashion. First, I will examine the principles which Murray held to be eternally and universally normative. Next, I will consider examples of their application in particular historical circumstances. Finally, I will present Murray's distinction between the universal and the particular and his new synthesis which he deemed necessary given the changing political and historical conditions of human society in the twentieth century.

Murray's scholarly integrity impelled him to cast a critical eye on every existing articulation of the Church's teaching regarding the relationship between Church and state. In a final attempt to remain faithful to the spirit of his theological investigations, I too will cast a critical eye on Murray's work. Just as Murray listened, understood, and then evaluated the works of others in his numerous scholarly articles, so too will I attempt to listen to the voice of this great thinker, understand his thoughts, and then subject his work to critical reflection.

In this manner, I believe, one may best understand the true import of Murray's work. His life work is not a storehouse of quotations or a source of authority behind which contemporary aficionados may hide in security. John Courtney Murray's political project, quite to the contrary, is a challenge to lay bare the essential bases of a political theory in order to separate what is eternal and universal from the contingent elements of its applications in ever-changing historical circumstances.

Chapter 1

The Social Nature
of the Human Person

MURRAY'S EXPLANATION OF THE AMERICAN CATHOLIC'S TWO-FOLD obligation to both the Church and the state required the application of universal principles within a particular historical situation. Specifically, he faced the challenge of proposing a means whereby American Catholics could remain faithful to the centuries-old tradition of the Church within the context of a thoroughly modern political regime. Given the novelty of the American political system relative to the life of the Church, it is no wonder that many of Murray's contemporaries in the theological community and in the Vatican hierarchy would be skeptical of his theological innovation. He therefore began his scholarly investigations with a re-iteration of the first principles of Christian anthropology in order to convince his contemporaries that one could be a loyal American committed to the principle of religious liberty and simultaneously remain a Catholic faithful to the Church's authentic teaching regarding Church-state relations.

Murray located the source of his teaching in the writings of the fifth-century Pope Gelasius I, and thus began his effort to establish the normative value of religious liberty.

The Gelasian Thesis and its Historical Development

Murray began his analysis of the relationship between religion and politics by describing in abstract terms the social nature of the

1

human person. Central to his theory was the idea that it is "the nature of man . . . to be at once citizen and Christian and one human person."[1] By implication, then, all human persons possess an integrity of personality which includes a form of "dual citizenship"—i.e., citizenship in a particular political community as well as citizenship in the universal Christian community. This conception of the dualistic nature of the human person's social existence was firmly grounded in the Church's social doctrine, according to Murray, and its first great proponent was Pope Gelasius I.

Pope Gelasius I: *"Duo Sunt . . ."*

Murray always maintained the truth of the Catholic teaching that "there are upon earth two great societies"—i.e., the religious and the civil.[2] He located the first formulation of this statement of Catholic doctrine in a letter written in 494 A.D. by Pope Gelasius I to the Byzantine Emperor Anasthasius I. In this letter, the Pope wrote: "Two there are, august Emperor, by which this world is raised in sovereign fashion . . . the consecrated authority of the priests . . . and the lower part and [of] these two, the responsibility of the priests is so much the weightier."[3]

This brief statement formed the basis for what Murray considered the normative implications of the Gelasian Thesis. The principles he derived from the statement above include the corollary that there is a definite distinction between the authority of the Church and the power of the state and a consequent distinction between their respective fields of competence. He further concluded that while the spiritual authority of the Church possesses an inherent dignity which suggests its primacy over the temporal power of the state, the temporal power of the state also exists with legitimate autonomy in its own sphere such that it may rightfully command the Church's obedience in temporal matters. Finally, because each stands in need of the other, Murray indicated that there ought to be a harmonious relationship between Church and state.[4]

Murray expressed his appreciation for the historical significance of Gelasius' pronouncement when he stated that "in the whole sea of literature on the Church-state problem, there is no text that is more capital than this one."[5] Given the relative clarity of this principle and its corollaries, it would seem that all that remained for both Church and state would be the task of establishing a harmonious relationship between concrete ecclesiastical and political institutions which would reflect this social dualism. A brief examination of the principal struggles between the sacred and secular powers in the Middle Ages, however, will demonstrate the difficulty of this project even in a society that was relatively homogeneous in its cultural and religious dimensions.

Gregory VII's Application of the Gelasian Thesis

Though Murray argued that the dispute between Gregory VII and Henry IV was qualitatively different from those of later Popes and secular rulers, nevertheless he also acknowledged that this conflict represented the first major struggle between the spiritual authority and the temporal power in medieval society.[6] Without tracing the specific details of the conflict that had erupted between the Pope and the Emperor regarding the problem of lay investiture, suffice it to say that when the conditions of the controversy had become intolerable to both, Gregory excommunicated Henry in February, 1076 and (by releasing Henry's subjects from their oath of allegiance) attempted to depose him. Henry responded by denying the Pope's authority to depose him and, questioning the legitimacy of his election, demanded that Gregory vacate the See of Peter.

Murray stated that although this struggle was of great magnitude in its own day, it did not necessarily involve a disagreement over the principles of social dualism but rather over the mode of their application in a particular historical period. On the one hand, Henry proposed that the "*sacerdotium*" ought to secure the obedience of the people to their king as the ruler second in authority only to God. On the other hand, Gregory maintained the absolute right of the Pope to excommunicate any member of the Church, including the Emperor, even if such excommunication warranted the forfeiture of one's temporal office.

Clearly, Gregory and Henry had arrived at an impasse in their efforts to secure the application of the Gelasian Thesis. Though Henry relented and appeared (barefoot) before Gregory at Canossa in 1077 seeking absolution, additional political conflicts regarding the restoration of Henry to the throne led to the final diremption of the relationship between the leaders of the sacred and secular realms in 1080. At that time, Gregory once again excommunicated Henry, and Henry promoted the election of an anti-Pope to take the place of Gregory. Both men died before they were able to secure a true reconciliation.

In spite of the great personal, political, and spiritual tragedy that had been endured, Murray insisted that there had been no real departure from the original principles of the Gelasian Thesis. He claimed that both parties agreed on the existence of a real distinction between the sacred and the secular societies. The controversy that emerged was primarily the result of a lack of consensus regarding the application of principles and the extent of jurisdictional autonomy. The legitimacy of the principles of the Gelasian Thesis was never in question. Murray argued that there was no direct challenge to the idea of social dualism until conflict erupted between Boniface VIII and Philip the Fair.

Boniface VIII and the "Two Swords" Controversy

Given the undeniable historical existence of the great "Church-state" controversies in the Middle Ages, Murray was quick to eschew any effort to romanticize that period as a "golden age" of the *Respublica Christiana*. He noted that the era actually represented a period in which the Church herself violated the Gelasian principle of social dualism. Further, he argued that "you will not find . . . in the Middle Ages a realization of the Gelasian Thesis that will stand forth somehow in flawless perfection." Rather, he claimed that as time progressed, "the medieval realization of the Gelasian Thesis—the one society, two swords idea"[7]—was actually an attempt to conflate the sacred and the secular societies in order to enable the spiritual authority to wield temporal power.

More than any other Pope, Boniface VIII was, in Murray's eyes, the spiritual leader who most flagrantly attempted to usurp power more appropriately exercised by the temporal ruler.[8] Although he noted that the "Two Swords" theory had been developing over a period of nearly 500 years before Boniface VIII promulgated the Bull *Unam Sanctam*,[9] he also argued persuasively that there can be little doubt that this Pope and this famous letter are justly indicted for promoting the most solemn statement of this aberration of the Gelasian Thesis.

The conflict between Boniface VIII and the French king Philip the Fair involved a dispute over the power of the king to tax the clergy in France. In 1296, Boniface, in the Bull *Clericos Laicos*, ordered the French clergy to refuse to pay any tax imposed on them by Philip. However, after Philip's vehement protest (which included the interruption of the exportation of gold and silver from the French bishops to Rome), Boniface agreed to relent, and a fragile truce was forged. The battle was joined once again, however, in 1301, when Philip had the Bishop of Parmiers arrested. In the Bull *Asculta fili*, Boniface responded by demanding the release of the bishop and threatening to excommunicate Philip. He also stated in quite explicit fashion his argument that the Pope was supreme over all kings on earth, and that the king therefore ought to acknowledge that he is indeed subject to the spiritual authority of the Church even in the exercise of temporal power.

In 1302, Boniface most explicitly stated his belief that Papal authority is supreme in all matters spiritual and temporal in the famous Bull *Unam Sanctam*. In that letter, he claimed that in the earthly social order "there are two swords, the spiritual and the temporal." He went on to claim, moreover, that "these are both in the power of St. Peter and the Church, the one to be used by the priest, the other by the king, but at the command ("*ad nutum*") of the priest." Further, "the temporal authority must be subject to the spiritual ("*spirituali subjici potestati*") [because] the spiritual power is superior in dignity to the temporal, and it has therefore authority to 'institute' the temporal."[10]

Philip was not persuaded by Boniface's theoretical statement of his authority, nor was he afraid of using force to demonstrate his own power over the Pope as he proved in sending an expeditionary force to Rome to capture Boniface. Although his soldiers refused to arrest Boniface and were eventually repelled by the Pope's allies, Philip nevertheless successfully avoided any serious challenge to his temporal authority and further eluded any spiritual sanctions from Boniface's successors upon the death of the latter. In fact, Pope Clement V later revoked those portions of *Clericos Laicos* and *Unam Sanctam* which might have been perceived as being injurious to the king.

The political defeat of Boniface VIII which marked the conclusion of this struggle effectively repudiated the practical viability of the "Two Swords" Theory. From Murray's standpoint, this event was not at all lamentable, however, because this theory was an aberrant application of the Church's teaching regarding the extent and limits of religious authority and political power. Clearly, in claiming that the Pope controls the "two swords" and merely delegates the temporal power to the king, Boniface had proposed a monistic scheme of social organization which was in sharp contrast to the Gelasian notion of social dualism. In usurping the legitimate authority of the king in the temporal realm, the Pope had claimed a measure of power which was not rightfully his. It was no more legitimate for the spiritual authority to claim a share of the temporal power than it is for the temporal power to claim the right to exercise spiritual authority. Murray pointed to the irony of the events surrounding the Pope's self-destruction when he stated that although Boniface VIII "thought he had written the charter of the medieval Christian Commonwealth in his great bull, *Unam Sanctam*—as a matter of fact, he had written its epitaph."[11] The task of re-stating the principles of social dualism and reclaiming the Gelasian heritage thus fell to future leaders of the Christian community.

John of Paris' Analysis of the Nature of the Sacred and the Secular Societies

This examination of the medieval effort to implement the principles of the Gelasian Thesis demonstrates the difficulty of descending from such abstract concepts as the idea of social dualism to the more concrete world of ecclesiastical and political institutions. Murray's search for a method to facilitate the harmonization of the sacred and secular societies in their institutional manifestations led him to a more detailed analysis of the origins, purposes, means, and ends of both societies.[12] It is ironic that in the midst of the religio-political turmoil of the middle ages Murray also located the works of John of Paris which were perhaps the greatest single source of wisdom regarding the practical application of the Gelasian Thesis.

The Spiritual Society

There is little dispute among those who belong to the Christian community that the Church presumes its origin in the will of Jesus Christ himself. This principle is an article of faith that John of Paris himself took for granted. According to Murray, John of Paris postulated that it was a revealed fact that "the spiritual (authority) is immediately from God."[13]

Knowing the origin of this spiritual society, it follows that one ought to determine its purpose or function. In John's political theory, Murray found an unambiguous assertion that the spiritual authority is entrusted with the responsibility "of leading man and society . . . [to] eternal life." The purpose or function of the spiritual authority is therefore the "dispensation of the sacraments which contain the grace whereby we are set on the way to eternal life."[14]

Murray next proceeded to an analysis of the means which enable the spiritual authority to fulfill its purpose of leading all people to eternal salvation. In the work of John of Paris, he found an articulation of six "component powers" which are "singly and solely spiritual in character" and which are the exclusive domain of the spiritual authority. These means include: 1) the power to consecrate the sacraments; 2) the power to administer the sacraments, especially penance; 3) the authority to preach the gospel; 4) the power to impose penalties for spiritual offenses; 5) the power to distribute ecclesiastical offices; and 6) the power to require from the faithful what is necessary for the support of the Church.[15]

Having determined the origin, function, and means of the spiritual society, Murray then considered its final end. He immediately noted that John of Paris taught that the ultimate end of the spiritual society was "a supernatural end which is eternal life."[16] The final end of the spiritual society would be realized, then, when all of God's people experienced eternal life at the *parousia* which would occur, as the Evangelists say, at an hour that "no one knows . . . but the Father" (Mt 24:36, Mk 13:28, Lk 21:29).

Murray claimed that John of Paris had offered a description of the nature of the spiritual society which was entirely consonant with authentic Church doctrine. By appropriating John of Paris' theory of the origin, purpose, means, and end of the spiritual society, Murray considered himself to have adopted an expression of the Church's teaching which was in accord with that articulated in the patristic age by Gelasius I.

The Temporal Society

Just as Murray relied on the works of John of Paris to provide a detailed analysis of the nature of the spiritual society, so he also described the nature of the temporal society with reference to the works of this medieval thinker. Murray found in this source ample material to support his belief that the temporal society, like its spiritual counterpart, could trace its origins to the will of God as expressed in his Eternal Law.

According to Murray, John of Paris affirmed the Thomistic (and Aristotelian) notion that the temporal society finds it origin in the nature of the human person who is "naturally a political or civil animal."[17] Quoting John, Murray stated that its origin is "from the natural law and the law of nations."[18] He then concluded that "since it is 'by a natural instinct which is from God that men live in civil society (*civiliter*) and in community,' the *regnum* itself is from God."[19] This idea that the origin of the temporal society may be traced to the human person's natural inclination to a social life that is part of God's plan for Creation was most clearly expressed by John when he wrote that the temporal society's distinct power emanated immediately from God and not (as Boniface claimed) from the Pope.[20]

In his investigation of the purpose or function of this divinely ordained temporal society, Murray gleaned from John of Paris the principle that the temporal society functions as the agent that directs its citizens toward the goal of establishing justice, peace, and prosperity—i.e., toward the *summum bonum* of the natural world. In his role as custodian of the *imperium*, the king must be "justice animate and the guardian of what is just."[21] To the judgement of the temporal power, therefore, "there are committed all cases involving violation of the justice enshrined in human laws, whose observance is necessary for civil peace."[22]

Murray argued that the means available to the temporal power to fulfill its function included primarily the faculty of exercising the instruments of coercion denoted by the Latin term *imperium*. John of Paris implicitly recognized the secular nature of these coercive means when he spoke of the need for the "secular" arm (*brachium seculare*) to supplement the Church's efforts to punish heretics.[23] While Murray himself questioned the legitimacy of these efforts to repress heresy (see Chapter 3 below), he nevertheless located in John's writings a clear recognition that coercive force could only be applied by those who possess temporal power. The authority to implement spiritual sanctions resided exclusively within the institutions of the spiritual society.

Murray concluded his analysis of the nature of the temporal society by describing the ultimate end to which it aspired. He firmly established himself within the Aristotelian-Thomistic tradition when he appropriated John of Paris' statement that "the end of civil society is 'that good which can be achieved by nature, which is a life according to virtue.'"[24] From John of Paris, Murray also gained the insight that the end of the temporal society is indeed autonomous, and its actualization is therefore independent of the *telos* of the spiritual society. Without compromising the unified personal integrity of each individual, Murray recognized, with John of Paris, that "the civic life of virtue . . . 'has in itself the nature of a good and is desirable for its own sake.'"[25] If the function of the temporal power is to establish the justice, peace, and prosperity necessary to live this life of virtue, then its final end can be said to be the perfect realization of these goods.

Murray's analysis of the nature of the spiritual and temporal societies thus facilitated an easy comparison of the major characteristics of each. While his analysis of the works of John of Paris uncovered the theological and philosophical bases of his Christian anthropology, the important task of examining how the two societies ought to act in harmony nevertheless remained. In striking a balance between the competing claims of the spiritual and the temporal orders, Murray argued, the individual ought to experience their co-existence as naturally harmonious rather than as an interminable struggle between two equally desirable but ultimately incompatible moral ends. Murray found ample material in the works of John of Paris to support this claim, and so it is to his examination of John's description of the proper integration of the spiritual and temporal societies that we now turn.

Social Dualism—Principles for Implementation

In the dualistic structure of human citizenship described by Murray, the individual human person possesses rights and responsibilities as a member of both the sacred and the secular societies. However, their distinctive origins, purposes, means, and ends could conceivably place conflicting demands on the individual and sunder one's personal integrity. In the face of this potential internal psychic discord, Murray argued that the principles of *concordia* and the primacy of the spiritual would act as the means whereby the ethical demands of the two societies would be reconciled within the conscience of the individual. An examination of the theoretical statement of these principles therefore remains as the final element in this analysis of Murray's description of the social nature of the human person.

Concordia: The Concept of Harmony

While one of Murray's greatest contributions to the study of the appropriate relationship of religion and politics may be his detailed analysis of the characteristics of the sacred and secular societies, such an analysis would be of limited significance were it not complemented by a study of how the individual is to recognize the reality of social dualism and also integrate the imperatives of the two societies in a manner that is conducive to authentic human existence. To demonstrate, at least on a theoretical level, how such harmony, or *concordia*, is possible, Murray retreated from his "black and white" analysis of the nature of the two societies and instead focussed on the complex integration of the competing ethical demands of the sacred and the secular societies which produces numerous "gray" areas in which the spiritual and temporal orders are in tension, dialogue, and hopefully (though not always) cooperation. In developing his argument regarding the necessity of harmony or *concordia* between the sacred and the secular societies, Murray again returned to the writings of John of Paris as an authoritative voice in his effort to retrieve the sources of authentic Catholic teaching.

We have seen that John of Paris considered the origins, purposes, means, and ends of both the sacred and the secular orders to be independent and distinct. We should also note, however, that John conceived of both as ultimately deriving their existence from the will of God. Given the medieval conception of nature's inherent unity, harmony, and synchronicity, it therefore remained for John to explain how the human institutions established in the sacred and secular societies could effectively manifest this orderly vision of creation.

In his effort to establish the theoretical possibility of *concordia*, John of Paris developed the notion of *indirect power* as a means of explaining the nature of the sacred society's influence on temporal affairs. According to John, it was inevitable that the spiritual authority would play an influential role in the temporal realm because by virtue of their teaching authority, bishops and priests "indirectly have a power in temporalities inasmuch as they lead men to penance and the restitution of stolen property, and to the largesse of temporal goods in accord with the demands of the order of charity."[26] Murray noted that in this articulation of the Church's teaching authority, John correctly acknowledged that the actions of the spiritual authority have temporal effects. John also recognized that the Church's direct action, whatever its indirect consequences, must primarily and exclusively be confined to the exercise of its spiritual authority. From John's writings, Murray therefore concluded that the Church's "action is a genuine means of directing the temporal processes, but a means proper to the order in which the Church exists, the spiritual order."[27]

Placing John's writings in their historical context, Murray noted that it was in the midst of the conflict between Boniface VIII and Philip the Fair that John asserted that "even the prince is subject to this [spiritual power] inasmuch as 'the prince has from the Pope and the Church his teaching about faith.'" What is more significant for the creation of harmony between the two societies, however, is the prince's recognition of the fact that although the Pope's "teaching cannot be without effects on his princely rule, at the same time . . . it is no threat to his legitimate independence."[28] Murray would extract from this historical example the re-affirmation of the Gelasian principle that the autonomy of the two societies and their operational integration were not mutually exclusive.

Murray considered John of Paris a truly judicious voice in the dialogue oriented toward the establishment of a harmonious relationship between the sacred and the secular societies. He noted that John of Paris "does not say that the Church has 'an indirect power,' but that the Church 'indirectly has a power,' which is more correct." Murray personally appropriated John's political theory when he wrote that in the effort to establish an existential *concordia*, "it is not to be thought that the Church has two powers, one direct, the other indirect; actually she has only one power, which is purely spiritual, but which indirectly operates temporal effects."[29]

The Primacy of the Spiritual in the Christian Conception of Politics

Despite the logical quality of distinguishing between the human person's spiritual and temporal nature and the apparent possibility of creating conditions under which the institutions of the sacred and secular societies would be capable of cooperating to advance the goals of each, the realistic critic of such a social arrangement would argue that conflict between the two societies would be inevitable given the human inclination to dispute the best manner of ordering their concrete relationship even in cases where there is consensus regarding the necessity of *concordia*. Murray was well aware of such a tendency to discord, and he was fully prepared to admit that a fundamental value judgement was necessary to preempt the psychic paralysis which might result were an individual forced "tragically" to choose between these values and ends. He readily found a solution to this dilemma, however, in the Gelasian Thesis. Specifically, he claimed that Catholic social thought from its inception held that despite the inherent dignity of the temporal realm, the supernatural ends of the spiritual society ought always to be given primacy in the resolution of value conflicts.

Given the tragic quality of the conflicts that had erupted during the Middle Ages when both the sacred and secular orders attempted to assert some form of control over each other, Murray was very careful in his definition of this concept of "primacy." He strongly affirmed the principle that "this primacy does not imply that the temporal power is somehow instrumental to the proper ends of the spiritual power or the Christian people." He also noted that the concept of "primacy" does not "have *per se* connotations of an ecclesiological jurisdiction *over* the temporal." Rather, "primacy *per se* asserts superior dignity," which is derived from its existence as "the unique means and milieu of man's eternal salvation, which as such claims the primacy over the order of man's terrestrial life and all its social forms."[30]

The influence which the spiritual authority may exercise in the temporal realm, however, is limited, as we have seen, to the indirect power of forming the consciences of those who would wield the power of ruling the secular society. As he had turned to the works of John of Paris to understand the teaching of the Church in the other aspects of his social theory, so Murray again sought the wisdom of this author in developing his twentieth century articulation of the Gelasian notion of the primacy of the spiritual.

John of Paris was of course a great expositor of the idea of the primacy of the spiritual. John's writings are particularly useful in the development of this idea because he affirmed the principle of the primacy of the spiritual while simultaneously rejecting the practical manner in which the spiritual leader of his day, Boniface VIII, attempted to exercise this authority. It is in his distinction between the theoretical principle and its practical abuse by his contemporaries that Murray located the true genius of John of Paris. It was John's great accomplishment, he wrote, "to set forth . . . the supremacy of the spiritual power" while at the same time "analyz[ing] at length the autonomy of the kingly power and . . . refut[ing] at still greater length the theories that diminished this autonomy in consequence of a failure exactly to delimit theological principle and justly to estimate political right."[31]

According to Murray, John of Paris considered the theoretical primacy of the spiritual to be "all too obvious" to merit sustained philosophical justification. As we have seen, within the historical context of the Middle Ages, John took for granted that those who would read

his treatises would unanimously consent to the truth of "the revealed fact that the 'good life' in the earthly City is not man's
highest end, . . . [for] he is further 'destined to a supernatural end
which is eternal life.'" John went so far as to insist that ultimately the
primacy of the spiritual order is manifested by the fact that even
though "the earthly power is immediately from God, . . . it is directed
to the blessed life by the spiritual power."[32] Thus, while John insisted
that the spiritual authority may only indirectly claim a power to influence temporal affairs, he was also quite explicit in his conclusion that
when the values of the two societies appear to conflict, individuals
must recognize the primacy of those of the spiritual society.

It was this recognition of the primacy of the spiritual which, at
least on the theoretical level, enabled Murray to establish some criterion which would foster the harmony or *concordia* between the sacred
and the secular societies which John of Paris envisioned as the logical
outcome of the implementation of the principles of the Gelasian Thesis. It is also out of this tradition of social and political thought that
Murray drew the basic assumptions upon which he would build an
American Catholic political theory for the twentieth century. As he
continued to lay the groundwork for a positive construction of the
ethical and theological bases of the idea of religious liberty, Murray
proceeded to investigate modern efforts to apply the principles of the
Gelasian Thesis. Chapter 2 considers these applications as constitutive
of the context within which Murray would begin his articulation of the
appropriate relationship between the sacred and the secular societies in
the twentieth century.

Glossary

auctoritas: the spiritual authority of the Church.

concordia: "harmony"; the integration of the institutions and imperatives of the spiritual and temporal societies in a manner conducive to authentic human existence.

Divine Law: God's direct revelation of his will for human persons communicated through the Scriptures and the Tradition of the Church.

"Duo sunt . . .": "Two there are . . . "; first words of Pope Gelasius I's statement of the Church's doctrine regarding the relationship of the spiritual and temporal societies.

Eternal Law: the rational governance of all of Creation by God who is its Author.

Gelasian Thesis: term used by John Courtney Murray to designate the essential elements of Catholic doctrine regarding the relationship between the spiritual authority of the Church and the temporal power of the state as he derived them from the teaching of Pope Gelasius I (492-496).

Lay investiture: medieval practice in which a bishop at his installation would receive the insignia of his office (i.e., his staff and ring) from a feudal lord in a manner that compromised the freedom and autonomy of the Church.

Natural Law: the participation of human persons in God's governance of Creation through their inclination toward actions and the end which is proper to them by nature.

potestas: the temporal power of the state which compels by virtue of force and coercion.

Primacy of the spiritual: the principle which recognizes the dignity of the human person's supernatural end and establishes the superiority of the normative demands of the spiritual society to those of the temporal society in cases in which there is an apparent conflict between the two.

Respublica Christiana: term used to designate the medieval relationship between the spiritual and temporal societies in which the Church temporarily enjoyed efficient organization and powerful influence in the affairs of the temporal society.

sacerdotium: "the priesthood"; in a general sense, the clergy as they used their teaching authority to lead the people.

Social dualism: term used to designate the Christian understanding of the human person's participation in the life of both the spiritual and temporal societies.

Spiritual society: the total complex of human relationships instituted in and through Jesus Christ and organized for the purpose of leading human persons, through the proclamation of the Gospel and participation in the sacramental life of the Church, to the supernatural end of eternal life with God.

Temporal society: the total complex of organized relationships which human persons are naturally inclined to form in order that they might cooperatively and collectively promote a life of virtue in pursuit of the ends of justice, peace, and prosperity.

"Two Swords" Controversy: term used to designate the political struggle between Pope Boniface VIII and the French king Philip the Fair regarding the relationship between the authority of the Church and the power of the state. Boniface believed that both religious and political power (the "two swords") resided in the Church, and that the state wielded political power only due to a grant of such power by the Church.

Discussion Questions

1. What are some concrete political issues that present Christians with an apparent conflict between their political values and their religious convictions?

2. What criteria do Christians use to determine the appropriate course of action to take when there appears to be an unavoidable conflict of religious and political values?

3. To what extent do people in contemporary society recognize the superiority of spiritual goods over temporal goods? Give some examples to support your assertion.

4. Do you agree with the statement that the conflict between Boniface VIII and Philip the Fair did not involve a challenge to the principles of social dualism but rather a dispute over the best manner of implementing those principles? Why or why not?

5. Should a society that is religiously homogeneous organize itself politically according to the "Two Swords" model with the civil ruler(s) governing at the discretion of the religious leader(s)? What are the strengths and weaknesses of this form of social organization?

6. To what extent should the state be permitted to restrict the activities of the Church and other religious groups? Does the exercise of this regulatory power imply the "reverse" of the "Two Swords" theory, i.e., that the Church enjoys freedom only to the extent to which the state grants it?

7. Does John of Paris' distinction of the origins, purposes, means, and ends of the spiritual and temporal societies clarify or confuse your understanding of the relationship between religion and politics?

8. Give some specific examples of the existence of harmony or *concordia* between the spiritual and temporal societies in today's world.

9. Give some examples of the absence of harmony or *concordia* as manifested in conflicts between spiritual and secular values in the public life of this country.

Chapter 2

Modern Applications of the Gelasian Thesis

IN THE PRECEDING CHAPTER, I EXAMINED MURRAY'S ANALYSIS OF THE social nature of the human person. This analysis accounted for the co-existence of the sacred and secular societies and the need for both spiritual and temporal rulers to promote the harmonious integration of the two societies as they simultaneously take account of the complex structure of human social existence. It also examined various attempts to implement the principles of social dualism within the historical context of the middle ages.

In this chapter, I will examine Murray's critique of some modern efforts to establish an appropriate relationship between Church and state. In examining this critique, I will attempt to show how Murray insisted that the Gelasian principle of social dualism is the only legitimate starting point in the attempt to formulate an authentic teaching regarding Church-state relations. I will also demonstrate how Murray was a theorist who attempted to preserve what was universal in such abstract imperatives as the primacy of the spiritual while simultaneously maintaining a sensitivity to the equally imperative demands of what Justice Oliver Wendell Holmes once called "the felt necessities of the time."[1]

This study of Murray's critique of the application of the Gelasian Thesis in the modern context will consider his analysis of the political theology of both Robert Bellarmine (1542-1621) and Leo XIII.

18

Murray's Critique of Bellarmine's Political Theology

Murray began his critique of the modern articulation of the Gelasian Thesis in two articles analyzing St. Robert Bellarmine's theory of the Church's indirect power to exercise authority in the temporal realm.[2] In a manner consistent with all of his theological investigations, he set out what he believed to be Bellarmine's faithful witness to the Church's teaching before he began his own critique of the danger of confusing universal principles with their historical application.

Murray affirmed the truth of Bellarmine's belief that "there is in the Pope a power in regard of temporal affairs." He further concurred with Bellarmine's statement that "this is not a matter of opinion but of certainty among Catholics." Finally, he also insisted on the wisdom of Bellarmine's observation that "there is no lack of disputes over what kind and manner of power it is."[3]

These lingering "disputes" are due to the nature of the Church's political theology. "Political theology," according to Murray's definition, is the Church's "theology of her relations to the temporal order." This theology may be considered in terms of the two aspects of which it is composed: 1) "premises and principles . . . [which] are indeed firm and unchanging, resting on foundations that stand outside time and the corrosiveness of political change;" and 2) "the contingencies and relativities of the political order, whose institutionalization is constantly dissolving." "Political theology," therefore, is never a "fully 'closed' theology" because its first principles (though themselves universal, eternal, and immutable) always find their embodiment in the ever-changing political institutions which manifest themselves in the contingent environment of different historical periods.[4]

By praising Bellarmine for having set out a political theology appropriate "in his own day," Murray demonstrated his abiding commitment to the Catholic tradition. However, he maintained his integrity as a true critic by pointing out that although Bellarmine's

> theological systematization . . . was an historical achievement of the first order, immensely influential in his own time, and regarded as a classic ever since, . . . [nevertheless,] his achievement was only historical, not eternal. He did not 'fix' the political theology of the Church in its final form.[5]

According to Murray, in his statement of abstract principle, Bellarmine manifested a considerable fidelity to the Church's authentic teaching as articulated through the medieval period from the age of Gelasius I to that of John of Paris. Just as John was willing to admit that the Church had only an indirect power in the temporal realm, so Bellarmine also wrote that "the Pope as Pope directly and immediately has no temporal power but only a spiritual power"; it is only "by reason of his spiritual power [that] he has . . . indirectly a power in temporal things."[6] This re-affirmation of the central tenet of the Gelasian Thesis proved to be somewhat specious, however, for, as Murray noted, Bellarmine's estimation of the possible uses of this indirect power threatened to blur any meaningful distinction between the principles articulated by Gelasius I and John of Paris and those of the "Two Swords Theory" of Boniface VIII.[7]

Bellarmine claimed that although the Pope had no direct power to depose kings, he could, nevertheless, "change the royal power . . . if this be necessary for the salvation of souls." Although he denied the Pope's ordinary authority to "make, . . . confirm, or invalidate the laws of princes," he did grant that the Pope "can do all these things if such action is necessary for the salvation of souls." Finally, though he insisted that "the Pope as Pope cannot by ordinary jurisdiction decide civil cases," he also allowed that "in a case in which this is necessary for the salvation of souls, he can assume civil jurisdiction."[8] Given great latitude in determining what is "necessary for the salvation of souls," the Pope might easily assume so prominent a role in the activities and affairs of the secular realm that the distinction between the spiritual and temporal authority would be completely obliterated. Murray, keenly aware of the danger of granting the Pope direct power beyond his legitimate spiritual authority, quickly pointed out these theoretical inconsistencies in Bellarmine's thought.

"Seen in the decisive instances of its use," Murray wrote, "Bellarmine's indirect power appears as more than simply a spiritual power that extends itself into the realm of the political, . . . [for] in the course of its extension the power itself has ceased to be purely spiritual and become[s] formally temporal." Rather than correcting the idea that the Church has a direct power in the temporal realm, Bellarmine brought "it back in, considerably modified but substantially itself." Murray concluded that "Bellarmine's indirect power seems to be simply a direct power restricted to exceptional use."[9] This particular articulation of the Church's teaching *vis à vis* the relationship of religion and politics is therefore profoundly problematic in its foreseen implications.[10]

There are two possible explanations which may account for Bellarmine's failure to produce a political theology that was thoroughly consistent with the Gelasian Thesis. One is the often-overlooked fact that in appropriating principles of medieval political theory he over-estimated the degree to which the medieval period was the political idyll that some are wont to portray it to have been. The medieval period was actually an era of profound political struggle between spiritual and temporal rulers. As a result of the turbulence which characterized the period, the political theory of the age often reflected the simple desire to legitimate the *status quo* once a measure of harmony had been realized.

Since much of the political theory of this era reflected the imperfection (or worse, the failure) of the efforts to ameliorate the struggle between the two societies, it is safe to assume that medieval Christendom never experienced the institutionalization of an "ideal" relationship between religion and politics. Murray noted the failure of the medieval political society to perfectly embody universal principles in particular historical circumstances when he wrote that

> the principles that guided action became matter for reflection only as they appeared in the action itself; however, since the action was designed to meet the exigencies of the contingent social situation in which the two powers met (usually in conflict), the principles could only with difficulty be seen in their clarity and purity.[11]

One could thus reasonably object that, in appropriating the insights of his predecessors, Bellarmine might also have shared their predilection to confuse universal principles with their application in a particular historical period.

Beyond this fundamental problem of distinguishing the universal from the particular, Murray noted that Bellarmine (like many theorists of the medieval period) also failed to appreciate the full implications of the Gelasian Thesis with regard to the autonomy of the temporal society.[12] While it may indeed be true that "it is Bellarmine's singular merit . . . that he newly organized and revivified the Thomistic philosophy of political power as natural in origin, temporal in end and field of competence," it is no less true that his "polemical preoccupations did not permit him to go deep into the idea that . . . the finality of the temporal power . . . is a genuine finality in its own right," and that this finality establishes a large measure of the "autonomy of the State."[13]

Because much of Bellarmine's work was indeed apologetic and directed toward the refutation of the notion of royal absolutism, it is no wonder that he would feel no inclination to develop a political theology that emphasized the (relative) autonomy of the temporal power.[14] It is likewise understandable, given Bellarmine's familiarity with the writings of theorists who were themselves embroiled in numerous conflicts between spiritual and temporal rulers, that he would be inclined to take his stand on behalf of the freedom of the Church in its effort to assert its authority to lead all people to salvation as it was so ordained by God. However, as twentieth century political theorists, we must ultimately insist that the influence of these historical factors necessarily mitigates the transtemporal value of Bellarmine's work.

To elaborate just briefly on the historical context of Bellarmine's polemics, it must be remembered that he grounded his arguments against royal absolutism in a political theory that was itself a reflection of an immature political society. Specifically, his claims regarding the right of the Church to exercise temporal power were first stated in the Middle Ages when "there were no effectively organized political institutions that could contrive to keep the monarch subject to law, or do away with him if he became a tyrant." According to Murray, Bellarmine was merely defending the Church's right "to step into a political vacuum, created by the absence of a political institution able to constrain the monarch to obedience to law." His instinctive conservatism in the face of the temporal power's challenge to the Church's authority may have indeed hindered him from seeing "how much of the hypothetical, the contingent, the relative, it [i.e., his political theology] embodied." In the end, however, despite "his defense of the permanent and absolute principles on which that theology rests," and despite the doctrinal advance "he effected . . . within the

Church herself by finally disposing of the confusions and ex-aggerations of the hierocrats,"[15] Bellarmine's success was limited by his failure to distinguish what was universal in the Church's teaching from what is historically contingent.[16]

Murray concluded that in developing his theory of "indirect power," Bellarmine "seems to have identified the principle itself with the contingent modes of its applications." True to the nature of some forms of the medieval enterprise of which he was anachronistically a part, Bellarmine fell prey to that tendency "of the medieval mind to regard as absolute what was only relative."[17]

Murray was thoroughly appreciative of both the strengths and weaknesses of Bellarmine's political theology. Though he was en-amored of the controversialist's thorough-going Thomism, in the end, his scholarly integrity compelled him to be critical of Bellarmine's failure to recognize the degree to which historical circumstances influ-enced his own articulation of the principles of the Gelasian Thesis. In a bit of understatement, Murray noted that "were he writing it today, [Bellarmine's] treatise, 'On the Power of the Pope in Temporal Af-fairs,' would have to wrestle with a vastly enlarged and complicated problematic, and make much more extensive use of the Thomistic con-cept of the state."[18]

Murray judged the works of all polemicists by critically examin-ing the distinction between universal principles and their historical ap-plication. In the present case, he noted that to a very significant de-gree Bellarmine's political theology embodied "the direction and cor-rection that were proper to that historical realization which he found in his books." However, "this historical realization, for all its splendor . . . was not in all its details the incarnation of absolute divine inten-tions with regard to the relations between [the] spiritual and temporal" societies. As in every effort to create harmony between the claims of the spiritual and the temporal, there were in Bellarmine's works "con-tingent, relative, time-conditioned elements. And the element of the contingent in it necessarily impart[ed] an element of contingency to the construction Bellarmine erected on it."[19]

Murray's Analysis of the Teaching of Leo XIII

Murray approached his study of the political theology of Leo XIII with the same spirit of respectful criticism that characterized his study of the works of Robert Bellarmine. In many ways Murray considered Leo to be a truly faithful expositor of the authentic principles of the Gelasian Thesis. However, due to his commitment to an ideal of scholarly integrity, he could not accept all of Leo's *corpus* as the final expression of the Church's teaching regarding the appropriate relationship between religion and politics. We must therefore first examine Leo's "modern" articulation of the Gelasian Thesis on the level of principle, and then consider how he proposed to apply these principles in the historical circumstances in which he lived. At that point, I believe it will become obvious that historical contingencies greatly influenced Leo's efforts to move from the level of theory to that of practice.

Leo's Statement of the Principles of Social Dualism

Murray believed that more than any other Pope of the modern era, Leo XIII succeeded in re-establishing the authentic principles of the Gelasian Thesis as signposts for the Church in her effort to establish the proper relationship between religion and politics. Leo explained his understanding of the dualistic structure of human social existence in a number of letters and encyclicals written between 1880 and 1902.[20] One may locate the components of the Gelasian Thesis in each of these works. However, the leading text in this series, according to Murray, is the encyclical *Immortale Dei*, and so it is to a consideration of this work that we will now turn.

Leo began *Immortale Dei* by affirming what Murray considered the first principle of the Gelasian Thesis, namely, the distinctiveness of the authority and competence of both the spiritual and temporal societies. He wrote that "God has divided the government of the human race between two powers, the ecclesiastical and the civil," and of these, "one of them is set in charge of divine things, the other of human things." Further, he wrote, "each of them is supreme in its own order."[21]

Leo also affirmed in *Immortale Dei* the other elements of the Gelasian Thesis which Murray had outlined. He indicated the primacy of the spiritual over the temporal when he wrote that because "the end to which the Church tends is by far the most sublime, so its authority is primatial. It cannot be considered inferior to civil government or in any way subject to it."[22] In reference to the inherent dignity and autonomy of the temporal society, Leo stated that "due regard must also be had of the excellence and nobility" of *both* powers. He further insisted that "those things which are ranged in the category of civil and political matters . . . should be under the control of the civil authority, since Jesus Christ gave the command that the things which are Caesar's are to be rendered unto Caesar, and the things which are God's unto God."[23]

Leo finally considered the need to establish that harmony between the spiritual and the temporal orders which Murray considered the fourth great component of the Gelasian Thesis. He noted that obviously "both powers rule over the same men, and occasions arise in which one and the same matter, in diverse ways, falls under the jurisdiction and judgement of both." For this reason, "it is necessary that a certain orderly relationship should obtain between the two powers."[24] How institutions within the two societies are to be arranged in order to promote this harmony, however, is a vexatious problem, and its solution, as we have seen, requires a better understanding of the exact origin, purpose, means, and end of each.

Leo took for granted that Jesus Christ himself was the Author of the spiritual society. His affirmation of this principle was almost ubiquitous in all of those writings which Murray labeled the "Gelasian texts." For example, in *Arcanum*, Leo spoke of Christ as "founder of the Church." In *Officio Sanctissimo*, he referred to Jesus as Son of God and Author of the spiritual society. Finally, he affirmed the divine origin of the spiritual society in both *Sapientia Christianae* and *Praeclara Gratulationis.*[25]

Leo explained the function or purpose of the spiritual authority when he wrote in *Immortale Dei* that its aim is "to put heavenly and eternal goods at the disposal of man." Beyond this general expression of the function of the spiritual authority, Murray also found in Leo's writings an elaboration of its specific role in the life of each person.

The purpose of the spiritual authority, Leo wrote in *Officio Sanctissimo*, is to act as "the single judge and mistress of truth." The spiritual power also assumes the function of "further[ing] among men the practice of virtue" in order to lead all "to their eternal salvation" (*Praeclara Gratulationis*).[26]

In his analysis of Leo XIII's Gelasian texts, Murray also found a statement of the Church's teaching regarding the means available to the spiritual authority for the fulfillment of its salvific purpose. Leo most clearly listed these means in *Officio Sanctissima* when he wrote that it is the exclusive responsibility of the spiritual authority to "teach Christian doctrine, administer the sacraments, perform divine worship, [and] establish and regulate the whole discipline of the clergy."[27]

Murray noted that Leo XIII also stressed the supernatural quality of the end proper to the spiritual society. Leo nowhere expressed this idea as clearly as he did in the 1884 encyclical *Nobilissima Gallorum Gens* in which he wrote that the spiritual authority would attain its proper end when it had fulfilled its responsibility to "lead men to the true blessedness for which we are made, an eternal blessedness in heaven."[28] Leo thus shared John of Paris' belief that the salvation of souls and the eschatological realization of the Kingdom of God represent the ultimate end or *telos* of the spiritual society.

In a similar fashion, it was not difficult for Murray to find further justification for his position regarding the divine origin of the temporal society in Leo XIII's works. For instance, in *Immortale Dei*, Leo wrote that "God has divided the government of the human race between two powers, the ecclesiastical and the civil." In *Sapientia Christianae*, referring to these two societies, he asserted that "God is the author of both," and in *Praeclara Gratulationis* he noted that God has "providentially set both the civil and the sacred power over the human community."[29]

Leo XIII likewise explained the proper function of the temporal power in the Gelasian texts to which we have already referred. In *Immortale Dei* he spoke of "the excellence and nobility" of the temporal power's purpose of providing "a sufficiency of earthly things"— e.g., justice, peace, and prosperity. Similarly, in *Sapientiae Christianae* he stated that since "it is the intention of nature that we should not simply be, but also be moral," it is therefore imperative that "the organized civil community . . . should allow [each person] to be a moral being . . . with sufficient assistance toward the perfection of [his or her] moral nature." According to Murray, this provision for "the tranquility of public order . . . is the proximate purpose" of the temporal power.[30]

Leo's teaching included a consideration of the means available to the secular power for the fulfillment of its divinely ordained purpose. He recognized the coercive nature of civil law, but his intention was not so much to proffer an analytical description of the nature of coercive power as it was to delineate the scope of its legitimate use. In fact, throughout the major texts in which Murray sought the crux of Leo's teaching, there are a greater number of examples of his desire for harmony between the spiritual and the temporal societies (and the laws and sanctions which pertain to them) than there are catalogues of the exact means of coercion available to each.[31]

Finally, Murray easily found in the Leonine texts a statement of the ultimate end of the temporal society. In speaking of this society, Leo wrote that "its proximate end is to ensure the temporal and earthly good of mankind" which is the human person's "perfection of his moral nature." With Aristotle, Aquinas, and John of Paris, Leo agreed that the *summum bonum* of earthly existence consisted precisely of a life of "knowledge and the exercise of virtue."[32]

Leo's Concept of *Concordia*

Unlike John of Paris who was writing in an era in which the spiritual authority needed to be restrained from usurping the power proper to the temporal order, Leo XIII recognized that in the nineteenth century the opposite threat to the incarnation of the Gelasian Thesis was present, i.e., the spiritual order was at risk of seeing its authority ignored or denied by the temporal power. In his analysis of the Leonine articulation of the concept of *concordia*, therefore, Murray focussed on this Pope's assertion of the limited competency of the temporal power.

So prominent is the concept of *concordia* in Leo's statement of the Gelasian Thesis that Murray remarked that this term "strikes literally the keynote of his pontificate."[33] In defining this concept, Leo envisioned a "dynamic harmony" or "orderly cooperation." The two societies were to foster mutual cooperation and promote the goals of one another in such a way that they preserved their uniqueness and yet also promoted the social development of the human person who belonged to both. According to Murray, Leo's understanding of the complementary existence and operation of the two societies produced two major conclusions regarding the duties of the sacred to the secular and vice versa. First, he derived the conclusion that "it is part of the duty of the Church to further by her own proper mode of action the ends of state and society, because these are human ends which apart from the spiritual aid of the Church . . . cannot be properly achieved." Likewise, "it is part of the duty of government and of all of the institutions of society to further by their own proper mode of action the end of the Church, . . . the achievement by men of the ultimate human purpose, salvation."[34] This statement of Leo's understanding of the concept of *concordia* is fraught with assumptions regarding the complex nature of human social existence, and therefore requires greater analysis if one is to comprehend the full import of Leo's teaching.

It would appear at first glance that Leo's statement of the mutual assistance of the sacred and the secular societies in the attainment of their respective ends at least blurs if not obliterates the distinctiveness of these ends and the exclusive competency of the various authorities within each social order.[35] In response to the difficulties present in Leo's political theology, Murray developed a sociological nomenclature which he hoped would eliminate the apparent inconsistencies in Leo's teaching and thus render his idea of *concordia* more intelligible.

Some Important Defintions. According to Murray, it is of paramount importance to distinguish the terms "civil society," "political society," "state," and "government." In this schema, "*civil society* designates the total complex of organized human relationships on the temporal plane . . . in view of the total cooperative achievement of partial human goods by particular associations or institutions." The end of civil society is, as we have seen, "a common good, *the* social good, pluralist in structure but somehow one, and therefore of a higher order than the goods of which it is, not the sum, but the unity."[36]

The experience of life in civil society includes a variety of forms of human interaction. In explaining this concept of civil society one author correctly notes that such a society "is composed of many diverse communities and groups: families, voluntary associations, colleges and universities, small businesses, corporations, labor unions, religious organizations and communities, and even governmental agencies."[37] In this definition of civil society, the spiritual authority exercises an *indirect* role in promoting the ends of the secular power, for in acting according to the evangelical law of love, the Church and the churches also satisfy many of the temporal needs of human society.[38]

Within this civil society, one can further differentiate the order of the *political society*: i.e., "civil society politically organized . . . for the common good [and] constituted a *corpus politicum* by effective ordination toward the political good, the good of the body as such."[39] Apart from its somewhat tautological definition, the term "political society" refers to the practical organization and coordination of the various orders (familial, cultural, educational, economic, and religious) within civil society. The term "political society" therefore appears to designate that organizational principle which enables civil society to recognize the unity inherent in the pursuit of the common good which is easily overlooked given the apparent plurality of partial goods pursued by individuals and institutions which compose subsidiary orders within civil society.

The designation of the *state* as one subsidiary order within society is also fundamental to an understanding of the concept of *concordia* which Murray derived from the works of Leo XIII. The "state," according to this definition, is simply "a set of institutions combined into a complex agency of social control and public service. It is a rational force employed by the body politic in the service of itself as a body."[40] The object or end of the state is therefore not to pursue a final end for itself. Rather, it exists to foster the ultimate end of a political society or body politic. The state's role is most properly to preserve public order, to provide that measure of "social control" necessary for the other orders of society to pursue those ends which contribute to the realization of the common good.[41]

The term *government*, the final concept integral to an understanding of the complex structure of human society, denotes simply the idea of "the ruler-in-relation-to-the-ruled . . . [and] the ruled-in-re-lation-to-the-ruler." In other words, "government gives concrete embodiment to the political relationship implied in the concept of the state."[42] "Government," like the concept of the "state" to which it is so closely allied, therefore represents another relationship subsidiary to the broader concepts of spiritual and temporal society. It must, for this reason, be relegated to the realm of the functional means which foster the higher ends of both the sacred and the secular societies.

Far from retaining the very clear distinctions between the spiritual and temporal societies which had been so prevalent in the earlier writings of Gelasius I and John of Paris, Murray's analysis of Leo XIII's teaching regarding the dualistic quality of human social existence portrays an utterly complex vision of human social organization. It also seems to imply that cooperation between the two orders requires some active promotion of the goals of one by the other and vice versa.

There is no doubt that Leo XIII was truly committed to the promotion of a harmony or *concordia* which recognized the fact that the "supernatural love of the Church and natural love of the country are twin-born loves, proceeding from the same eternal source . . . [and] that neither duty can conflict with the other" (*Sapientiae Christianae*).[43] It is also true, however, that such a harmony could only exist in a human family that recognized the complexity of its social existence and the operation of multiple orders within its otherwise dualistic social structure. An ideal of *concordia* could not be achieved within such a complex social system were it not for the final principle essential to Leo's articulation of the Gelasian Thesis—the principle of the primacy of the spiritual.

Like John of Paris, Leo also insisted that the recognition of the primacy of the spiritual was absolutely necessary if the harmony he so enthusiastically sought was to become a reality. Unlike John of Paris, however, Leo could not take for granted that his contemporaries assumed this primacy even on a theoretical level. He found it necessary to insist repeatedly that since "the end to which the Church tends is by far the most sublime, so its authority is primatial" (*Immortale Dei*).[44]

He based this teaching on the belief that "God established the Church in order that she might have under her care and attention and at her disposal those ultimate goods of the soul which are of incalculably greater value than anything found in nature" (*Officio Sanctissimo*).[45] His final bold proclamation of this primacy came when he wrote that "the Church is a society in her own right and is the most excellent society by reason of the excellence of the heavenly and immortal goods that are the object of her whole striving."[46]

Leo wrote these words in an historical environment in which the authority of the spiritual society was at risk of being denigrated and denied. It was in no position to usurp the temporal power of the institutions of the secular society. In fact, the greatest challenge Leo faced was the need to explain the proper institutionalization of the principles of social dualism in an era in which the Gelasian Thesis was ignored by those who sought the artificial separation of the naturally integrated religious and political dimensions of human social existence.

Leo's Condemnation of the Separation of Church and State

In his examination of the practical applications of Leo XIII's reinterpretation of the Gelasian Thesis, Murray pointed out that Leo's condemnation of the institutional separation of Church and state was at once the most prominent and problematic element of his teaching. So integral was this condemnation to Leo's social teaching that Murray devoted an entire article[47] and the greater portion of another[48] to an analysis of this element of his political theology.

According to Leo XIII, the principal enemies of the Church which sought to thwart its supernatural goals by destroying its human institutions were the "sects" in general and the Masonic Order in particular. Leo believed that these sects sought first to diminish the ability of the Papacy to exercise its spiritual authority in the temporal world. This would enable them to realize their ultimate goal of alienating whole societies from God. In order to accomplish these goals, the sects sought to obtain governmental power and to use that power to reduce the role of the Church in society.[49]

This enemy of the Church emerged in the nineteenth century European political environment in consequence of a more radical political experience—i.e., the theoretical repudiation of the Gelasian Thesis. According to Murray, Leo perceived the "sectarian" enemy to be the institutional manifestation of a monist conception of society which repudiated the traditional understanding of social dualism. Proponents of this "sectarian" monism attempted to usurp the authority of the spiritual realm and replace it with a "new political religion which sought to dictate the structure of society, to determine the ends of politics, ... and indeed to be the author of whatever salvation man might hope for."[50] The analysis of the Leonine texts which follows will clearly demonstrate the degree to which this Pope considered all of human society to be in great spiritual danger from this "alteration of the Christian structure of politics."[51]

Consistent with the position he took in those encyclicals quoted above, Leo criticized not only the immediate juridical problem associated with a separation of Church and state but also the philosophical denial of the principle of social dualism. That is to say, Leo XIII obviously considered it a grave evil that the Church's "properties [were] confiscated; [that] her freedom [was] restricted; [that] difficulties [were] thrust in the way of the education of aspirants to the priesthood; [that] the clergy [was] subjected to laws of exceptional severity; ... [and that] the religious congregations [were] dissolved and outlawed."[52] However, much more evil was the idea of social monism which fostered this juridical policy.

Leo condemned the continental form of separation of Church and state in numerous letters and encyclicals.[53] However, we may once again turn to *Immortale Dei* to find his clearest denunciation of what he considered the secularization of society. In this encyclical, Leo criticized the closed society-state in which the spiritual and temporal realms were subsumed in the hands of a government whose ends were solely immanent by nature. In such a society, he wrote, "the place in society accorded to the Catholic Church is on par with, or even inferior to, the place granted to associations of quite a different nature." Failing to recognize the dualistic structure of human citizenship, "civil officials on their own authority and at their own pleasure decide even those matters which are under a twofold jurisdiction [such as marriage and Church possessions]." This "separation" of Church and state actually represented an attempt to subordinate the Church to the state. Those who promoted this goal asserted that all of the Church's "rights and all her legitimate powers are possessed by her by the grant and grace of the secular government."[54] Leo thus imagined himself to be locked in a battle similar to that waged by Gregory VII or Boniface VIII. However, the opposition in the nineteenth century was not an absolute monarch but what J.L. Talmon would call a "totalitarian democracy."[55]

Leo continued his diatribe against this separation of Church and state because to him it represented a separation of the Church from society. "This kind of political order," he wrote, "is a deliberate policy either to drive the Church wholly out of public existence or to hold her bound and fettered to the regime." The practical consequences of such a social monism would include "the education of youth under exclusion of religion, the plundering and the destruction of religious orders, [and] the overthrow of the civil dominion of the Roman Pontiffs." In short, Leo believed that the tendency of continental liberal political theory was toward the establishment of totalitarian regimes "designed to put an end to the vigor of Christian institutions, to fetter the freedom of the Catholic Church, and to shatter all her remaining rights."[56]

Leo's critique of the separation of Church and state as he experienced it may be understood within the context of his fear that continental liberalism, taken to an extreme, fosters the establishment of a political environment in which "the absolutism of sovereignty . . . is now claimed by 'the people' in the Jacobin sense . . . by right of 'reason' which in the philosophy of the Enlightenment has become the divine majesty." He specifically regretted the tendency to view the "separation of Church and state as meaning the exile of God from Society." This exile, for Leo, did "not imply that a vacuum [was] to be left; actually, God [was] crowded out by an ideology which, under rejection of him, itself pretend[ed] to furnish the foundations and substance of society."[57]

Leo XIII: Two Concepts of Government

Leo XIII's condemnation of the separation of Church and state was not in any way intended to belittle the dignity of the secular power, nor was it an evangelical denunciation of the mundane or worldly. Rather, Leo merely sought: 1) the recognition of the dualistic nature of the human person's social existence; and 2) the protection of the freedom of the Church to participate in the formation of a public consensus regarding the nature of the common good. According to Murray, one could locate Leo's respect for the dignity of the state and his recognition of its important role in society in what he came to label Leo's "Two Concepts of Government."

In introducing the first of these concepts, Murray wrote that "Leo XIII assign[ed] to government a strictly political role with regard to the socio-economic order."[58] Relying on the text of Leo's famous encyclical, *Rerum Novarum*, Murray claimed that this "political" concept assigned the state the role of giving "assistance in general, . . . to undertake [no] more . . . nor go [no] farther than the remedy of evils or the removal of danger requires." The state exists to "protect . . . lawfully associated bodies of citizens but . . . [not to] intrude into their internal affairs." It also exists to come to the aid of the "unhappy multitude which has no security through resources of its own."[59] This statement of the political role of government appears to be consistent with what Murray earlier defined as the state's unique function of securing public order so that other institutions within society might be free to make their contribution to the realization of the common good.

Murray attempted to explain further the meaning of this "political" concept of government (which at once combined the seemingly incompatible ideas of governmental self-restraint and state intervention on behalf of those living on the margins of society) when he claimed that Leo's combination of the ideas of limited government and social welfare "preserve[d] him from the doctrinairism of both the Right and the Left." He located in this political concept of government "a healthy distrust of government when it begins to infringe on the freedom of society." However, he praised Leo's "sound respect for government when it acts within the limits of social necessities created by irresponsible uses or abuses of freedom." Murray summarized Leo's "political" concept of government by using a slogan he was to repeat often throughout his writings on Church-state relations: "As much freedom as possible, as much government as necessary."[60]

This "political" concept of government is very compatible with the classical conception of politics as understood by political theorists in the Aristotelian-Thomistic tradition. Murray noted that "the general principle upon which it is based is extremely broad"—i.e., the promotion of such public goods as justice, peace, and prosperity. The virtue which those who engage in this form of political life must cultivate is *prudence*. This virtue presupposes a knowledge of not only the abstract principles—justice, peace, prosperity—but also of "the existent state of balance or imbalance among social powers as well as a reasoned judgement with regard to the probable good or evil which would come from governmental action."[61]

It is important to remember that Murray noted that this "political" concept of government applied only to socio-economic institutions within Leo's political theology. Leo considered the law established to regulate the socio-economic order to be "a necessary instrument of social order," but he also recognized that "its value is limited . . . if it be regarded as a directive force, and still more limited if it be regarded as a coercive force." Leo assigned to government this strictly political role because human law is both inadequate as a redemptive force, and also subordinate to civic virtue, moral virtue, and religious faith as forces capable of promoting social order. Thus, although Leo upheld the dignity of the law enacted through the political process, "he regarded its value as secondary to conditions of religious and moral health in society."[62] It was therefore necessary to supplement this political concept with an understanding of the "paternalistic" role government plays in promoting the religious and moral health of society.

In Leo's political theology, strictly political questions "do not admit of any 'ideal' answer" because of the necessarily contingent nature of their solutions. However, once one transcends the level of the political and begins to consider the ethical bases of prudential judgements, one must recognize that "there is an objective distinction in value between ideas; some are true and some are false." This certainty of the existence of an objective moral order was the impetus for

Leo's belief that "there can be no such thing as governmental neutrality concerning the moral bases of society." In the ethical realm, the state "must positively favor and protect the human heritage against those who would dissipate it by the corrosion of doubt, denial, or cynicism."[63] This is the "paternalistic" concept which Leo believed ought to apply to the state's relationship with the cultural and religious orders of society.

Because Leo believed that "the freedom of man is rooted in reason," specifically "in that reflection of the Eternal Reason in nature which is the universal law," he denied the "Continental Liberalist concept of the public power as completely neutral in the face of truth and error." In his political theology, the state bears "responsibility for effective patronage of the true and good." It should "assume the patronage of truth" and "arrest the process which would lead to 'the ruin of society'" (although "only inasmuch as government is charged with responsibility for the public welfare").[64]

Leo did not intend to grant the state inordinate power within the cultural or religious orders in his description of its role in the preservation of the ethical bases of society. In fact, Murray claimed that had Leo been free to consider the relationship of the state to the order of culture solely in abstract terms, "he would have begun by laying down the classic medieval distinction between the *imperium* and the *studium*." Though it would have been somewhat anachronistic to apply these concepts to the nineteenth and twentieth century social climate, he might have made the claim that the *imperium* was the exclusive domain of the state whereas the *studium* was properly associated with the order of culture. In fact, Murray actually accepted this analogy when he conjectured that Leo XIII "would have said that the original responsibility for the order of culture rests on the *studium*, not on the *imperium*, [for] in principle, the order of culture, like the order of economic life . . . possesses its own autonomy and freedom in the face of political authority."[65] According to Murray, however, Leo was compelled to assert the need for governmental care for the order of culture as a reaction to the secularizing effects of the laicist theory of the state.

Murray further explained Leo's paternalistic concept of government when he wrote that within the order of religion, the state also possesses a positive obligation to foster the common good by promoting the spiritual growth of its citizens.[66] Since Leo believed that "those who rule over others rule only for one purpose, that they may further what is of advantage to society,"[67] he taught that governmental action on behalf of the common good included the duty to care for religion in a number of ways clearly indicative of a "paternalistic" concept of state authority. Murray noted that Leo had stated in *Immortale Dei* that at a minimum, the state must: 1) hold sacred the name of God; 2) extend favor to religion; 3) uphold religion by its good will; 4) protect religion with the authority and force of law; and 5) avoid establishing institutions and making administrative decisions contrary to the welfare of religion.[68]

The generality of these governmental duties is by all means obvious. Leo thus appears to have been speaking out only on a strictly *theoretical* level against the political philosophy which he believed to be dominant in European society in the nineteenth century. His primary intention was to counter the idea that religious faith and worship are "alien and of no interest" (*Immortale Dei*) to society. Recognizing the obviously polemical quality of these Leonine writings, Murray began the project of separating Leo's articulation of the timeless principles of social dualism from those contingent elements of his teaching which he intended solely as a response to the needs of his contemporaries.

Leo's Polemical Intentions

Murray affirmed the authoritative nature of Leo's writings on the relationship between Church and state immediately and forcefully in the final unpublished article in his Leonine series.[69] He also argued, however, that it is important to remember that Leo's writings were directed against both the religious and political philosophy which he encountered in nineteenth century European society. Specifically, Leo believed that his role as the leader of the institutional embodiment of the spiritual society compelled him to speak out against a religious philosophy of *conscientia ex lex*—i.e., the idea that "the absolutely autonomous individual conscience . . . recognized no law higher than its own subjective imperatives." Such a philosophy denied explicitly the Church's teaching regarding the existence of an objective order of natural and divine law which emanate from the Eternal Law of God.[70]

Leo also directed his encyclicals against a political philosophy of *principatus sine modo, sine lege*—i.e., the idea that government is "subject to no law higher than the will, itself lawless, of the Sovereign People."[71] In doing so, Leo acted not at all like many conservative theorists who sought to maintain the *status quo ante* the French Revolution. Rather, he countered the totalitarian tendencies of this political theory with a contemporary conception of the dualistic structure of human social existence that included an insistence on the circumscribed function and power of the state within the more complex and diverse orders of the temporal society.

Leo condemned the religious and political philosophy of continental liberalism because he abhorred its repudiation of the Church's traditional teaching regarding the complex structure of human social existence. The paternalistic concept of governmental care for religion which grew out of his polemical arguments represents an historical embodiment of the general principle that affirms the freedom and autonomy of the spiritual society and its institutional presence in the temporal society. Murray contended that Leo's political theology adequately defended the ancient principle of social dualism. He also argued that Leo never considered the idea of governmental care for religion to include as an element of Catholic doctrine the imperative that the Catholic Church be established as the religion of the state. In fact, the last article in the Leonine series seems to have been not so much a criticism of Leo's political theology as a repudiation of the effort of Murray's contemporaries to universalize what Leo himself considered to be historically-conditioned polemic.

In order to defend the authority of Leo's encyclicals while simultaneously criticizing those who sought to universalize the paternalistic concept of government, Murray sought to re-examine the context within which Leo wrote. Murray argued that Leo was engaged primarily in a political struggle with those who held fundamentally divergent visions of the ultimate ends of the human person. His was not a conflict regarding the merely proximate ends of politics. It is for this reason, Murray wrote, that Leo's encyclicals tend to display the characteristics of a defense of the freedom of the Church and the auton-

omy of the two societies rather than those of a vision of an ideal social organization characterized by the "unity which is peace."[72]

Murray argued that it would be a grave error to universalize that
which was historically conditioned in Leo's polemical writings. He
criticized the efforts of those theologians who attempted to transform
the exigencies of history into a body of theory which would be universally and eternally valid. He also criticized what he considered their
confusion of the process of making judgements in the contingent order
of law and politics with the epistemological process proper to the absolute order of ethical and theological truths. He argued, finally, that
unlike the twentieth century theologians who failed to recognize the
polemical nature of Leo's writings, Leo himself was careful to avoid
the fallacy that good human law can be universalized as true dogma or
that true dogma can find immediate embodiment in good human law.[73]

Having established the polemical nature of Leo's encyclicals,
Murray began to criticize his contemporaries' appropriation of what
they considered the universal principles of Leo's political theology.
This theological controversy would ultimately result in the censorship
of Murray's work and the temporary restriction of his investigations
into the appropriate relationship between religion and politics.

Glossary

Continental liberalism: political philosophy (especially prominent in France) notable for its espousal of the premises that all people are created in a condition of freedom and equality, that all truth, especially scientific and political truth, is accessible to human reason, and that religion, because its truth claims elude rational proof, is necessarily a private affair and therefore subject to exclusion from participation in the public life of a political society.

Hierocrats: those medieval theologians who attempted to subordinate the temporal power of civil rulers to the authority of the Church by alleging that such power belongs properly to the Church and is wielded by secular rulers only at the command of the Church.

imperium: "the power of commanding"; the ability of the state to coerce behavior among those who are subject to its power.

Indirect power: the ability of the Church to influence temporal affairs through the indirect consequences which proceed from its exercise of spiritual authority.

Political theology: a systematic reflection on or investigation into the Church's understanding of her relationship to the temporal order.

Royal absolutism: the centralization of political power—legislative, executive, and judicial—in the hands of a monarch who (in theory) is bound only by the demands of the natural law and (in practice) is accountable to no human power.

Social monism: a denial of the human person's simultaneous existence as a member of both the spiritual and temporal societies which is often manifested by the attempted usurpation of the authority or power proper to one society by the other.

studium: "devotion to learning"; the total complex of social institutions oriented toward the promotion of education and culture.

Totalitarian democracy: political society in which individuals freely cede the absolute right to determine the ends to be pursued in common to an omnicompetent state which they themselves have established.

Discussion Questions

1. How effective is the Church's "indirect power" in influencing the direction of temporal affairs today?

2. Do you agree with Murray's assertion that in Bellarmine's political theology the Church's "indirect power" was more than simply a consequence of the spiritual authority extending itself into the realm of the temporal but rather was an actual attempt on the part of the Church to exercise directly power that was properly temporal?

3. Are you generally optimistic or pessimistic about the possibility of even *approximating* an "ideal" relationship between Church and state in any place and time? What specific social conditions are conducive to achieving harmony or *concordia* between the spiritual and temporal societies?

4. Assess the competence of bishops, theologians, and political leaders to determine what is universally-valid and historically-contingent in the Church's political theology.

5. What political changes have taken place since the beginning of the 20th century which challenge theologians to articulate a political theology for the 21st century?

6. In your estimation, do most Americans understand the separation of Church and state to include the principle that religious ideas, teachings, and practices are to be excluded from the public life of this country?

7. Is there any room for a "paternalistic" concept of government within the American understanding of the role of the state in the life of its citizens?

8. Can you imagine any instance(s) in which the state ought to offer assistance in helping the Church achieve its properly spiritual ends?

Chapter 3

Murray's Initial Investigations of the Meaning of Religious Liberty in Catholic Social Thought

IN THE PRECEDING CHAPTERS, I HAVE DESCRIBED MURRAY'S INVESTIGAtion of historical efforts to establish an appropriate relationship between the spiritual and the temporal societies. I will now begin to outline in general terms the theory of his contemporaries who also sought to explain the normative principles for ordering Church-state relations. Then, having completed a survey of the development of Catholic political theology into the twentieth century, I will consider Murray's initial efforts to defend the principle of religious liberty as the best manner of incarnating the principles of social dualism in the political environment of the twentieth century.

The Political Theology of Murray's Contemporaries

Many of Murray's contemporaries attempted to claim Pope Leo's political theology as the basis for their own theological defense of the dual practices of religious establishment and governmental suppression of heresy. In the United States, John A. Ryan, George W. Shea, Francis J. Connell, and Joseph Clifford Fenton were the principal proponents of this articulation of Roman Catholic political theology. In

Rome, Alfredo Cardinal Ottaviani, Pro-Secretary of the Holy Office, also supported this articulation of Catholic teaching. These theologians formed the group of antagonists who both opposed Murray's efforts to promote the normative value of religious liberty and also effectively portrayed him as a thinker whose works had traversed the bounds of orthodoxy.

These theologians held the view that, in principle, Church-state relations ought to be ordered to project the ideal situation in which the Catholic Church would enjoy a certain status as the established Church in each particular country. In this ideal situation (the *thesis*), not only would the Catholic Church enjoy its establishment as the religion of the state, but it would also enjoy the favor of having the support of the government in its effort to suppress heresy and any and all other doctrines or ideologies which taught ideas contrary to its own beliefs. Thus, the *thesis* included the twin institutions of religious establishment and intolerance of dissent.

Where the *thesis* did not obtain and the Catholic Church existed either as a minority group or as one of many churches in a religiously pluralistic society, these theologians advocated the suspension of the normative principles of establishment and intolerance. In such a social environment, it remained for the Church to accept the equal toleration of all religious groups as the only expedient course of action. This *hypothesis* situation was evil in principle according to these theologians. However, they accepted such religious toleration as the lesser of two evils (as compared to religious persecution), and they acknowledged the practicality (but *not* the normative value) of the principle of religious liberty in religiously pluralistic countries such as the United States.

These theologians were extraordinarily consistent and unwavering in their commitment to the preservation of this theory as the authentic statement of Catholic teaching *vis à vis* Church-state relations. In his work on Murray's contribution to Church-state theory,[1] Thomas T. Love ably demonstrated that Ryan, Shea, Connell, Fenton, and Ottaviani all agreed on the fundamental assumptions necessary to establish the *thesis/hypothesis* distinction as the authentic expression of Catholic Church-state theory.

Initially, they all maintained the truth of the proposition that "there is only one true Church or religion," namely, the Catholic Church. Further, given the Church's role in the salvation of souls, they also held that "the state must aid the Church positively and defend it from all attacks." They then came to the conclusion that, by virtue of its *unique* role in the salvation of souls, "only the Catholic Church is to have full religious liberty."[2]

The second portion of the theory which these theologians upheld included the tendentious notion that "error has no rights." If it is true that the Catholic Church is the only true religion, then "all other so-called religions are in error, and error does not have the same right as truth." This was not to be interpreted as denying the individual's freedom of conscience, but rather as denying the right to oppose publicly that which is integral to the promotion of the public good—i.e., the truth of the Catholic faith. These theorists believed that "individual persons are . . . free to be in error, but such persons are not to be permitted to gather with others of similar error and to propagate error."[3]

According to Murray's contemporaries, once it is determined that the majority in a given nation accepts the truth of the Catholic faith, it becomes incumbent upon them "to oppose the external and public freedom of those holding different religious beliefs." That is to say, they are to promote the establishment of the Catholic Church as the "religion of the state"[4] to the exclusion of the public existence of all other Churches and religious organizations, and they are to enlist the active support of the state in the repression of heresy. If however, Catholics are in the minority, "they are to ask for religious freedom" as a "rationally expedient" principle until a future time . . . [when] the Roman Catholic Church will be able to establish itself in its proper preferential status."[5]

According to Love, these theologians, despite their apparent yearning for the twin institutions of establishment and intolerance, nevertheless agreed that the construction of such a "Catholic state" in the future was practically improbable. The *thesis* represented such a idyllic Christian commonwealth that it became apparent that its realization was "almost unimaginable, even in the so-called 'Catholic' lands."[6]

Murray believed that the practical implausibility of achieving the "Catholic *thesis*" was not sufficient to allay the concern of those Americans who objected to the denial of the normative value of the principle of religious liberty. He also sought to discover the true status of the *thesis/hypothesis* distinction as authentic Catholic doctrine. While he never questioned the truth of the Catholic faith, Murray did investigate the normative value and the moral significance of the practices of religious establishment and governmental repression of heresy.

Murray began his critique of the political theology of his contemporaries by studying the ethical value of the principle of religious liberty. His investigations then led him to consider the authoritative nature of various papal pronouncements as well as the doctrinal status of his contemporaries's appropriation of the teachings of these Popes. Murray encountered strong resistance to his critical work within the institutional Church, and his religious superiors, under pressure from Cardinal Ottaviani and others, soon admonished him to refrain from publishing articles and speaking publicly on the subject of Church-state relations.

In the remainder of this chapter, I will examine Murray's criticism of his contemporaries' explanation of the relationship of religion and politics as well as his initial arguments in defense of religious freedom. I will then consider in Chapter 4 the further development of his statement of the normative value of the principle of religious liberty both during and after the Second Vatican Council.

Murray Begins to Address the Church-State Issue

Murray's explanation of the normative value of religious liberty did not reach its full maturity until nearly twenty years after its inception. As we have seen, his project involved more than a mere perusal of the pronouncements of the Popes of the nineteenth and twentieth centuries. It actually included the resurrection of the wisdom of the fifth-century Pope Gelasius I, the subsequent restoration of the authentic principles of social dualism, and the eventual critique of the manner in which others had applied these universal principles in particular historical circumstances.

J. Leon Hooper has convincingly demonstrated that Murray's argument supporting the normative value of religious freedom emerged and matured over a twenty-two year period from 1945 until his death in 1967. He has stated that one can identify eight unique stages in the development of Murray's thought.[7] I will now begin to examine these stages of development in order to demonstrate the painstaking and thorough quality of Murray's effort to defend the normative value of religious liberty. I will also indicate, when appropriate, the points at which his ideas and writings drew him into direct conflict with his contemporaries whose opposition and influence would impede the publication of some of his works prior to the Second Vatican Council.

The Manualist Argument (1945-1947)[8]

Murray initially chose to investigate the problem of religious freedom because he believed it to be "a political problem of the first magnitude" which by 1945 had become "a matter of international concern."[9] He further believed that while Catholics and Protestants carried on an argument over the theological bases of religious liberty, secularism loomed as a force capable of "evacuating the concept . . . of all ethical content," and totalitarianism threatened to destroy "the concept itself, whatever its content."[10] Given the urgency of the problem and the theological divisions among Christians themselves, Murray attempted to analyze the question of religious liberty first in terms of its ethical dimension—the plane on which he believed there could be an "important measure of agreement" between Catholics and Protestants. He then planned to develop a theological justification of religious freedom upon which Catholics and Protestants could "agree to disagree." Finally, he hoped to develop a political basis for religious liberty which would promote "harmony of action . . . in virtue of the agreement previously established on the ethical plane."[11]

The ethical justification of the concept of religious liberty was, by Murray's own admission, "abstract in a twofold sense." It was abstract in that it considered simply "the *nature* of the elements involved" and also because it considered the issue in a manner that was "purely philosophical . . . [and] solely in terms of human reason."[12]

In his explanation of the ethical basis of religious liberty, Murray first posited the existence of a God from whom emanates a natural law which reason can discover and which establishes "man's essential duties towards God, himself, and his neighbor." He also posited the existence of a political society—a realm in which human law was also morally binding on the individual so long as it was not violative of the principles of the natural law. In this schema, the free human person confronted the *objective* precepts of natural and human law. These laws were then mediated to the individual in both cases by *conscience*—"a practical judgement of reason whereby a man judges of the morality of a concrete act." In the exercise of practical reason, then, conscience is "the proximate *subjective* norm of action."[13]

Murray thus attempted to construct his first defense of the concept of religious liberty in terms of the rights of conscience. Specifically, he sought to determine the normative value of religious freedom by analyzing the rights and duties which the human person and the state possess by virtue of their relationship to God.

Murray noted that "over against God and the eternal order of reason which He has established for the government of his rational creatures, conscience has no rights, but only the duty of unlimited obedience to God's known truth and will."[14] This is true of the human person's relationship to God in both its individual and social dimensions.

As an individual, the human person is obliged to:

1) search for the truth about God; . . . 2) worship God as God wishes to be worshipped; . . . 3) foster in himself a clear and right conscience; . . . 4) protect and develop the natural institutions of the family and civil society; . . . and 5) assist his neighbor toward the knowledge of God and towards obedience to the law of God.[15]

All human persons, with their neighbors naturally organized as part of a state,[16] have the obligation to

1) acknowledge God as . . . author [of the state], to worship Him as He wills to be worshipped, and to subject . . . [the state's] life and action to His law; . . . and 2) promote public religion and morality as essential elements of the common good.[17]

This second obligation includes the duty to

a) establish a regime of civil law that will confirm and sanction the juridical order of natural rights and duties; . . . b) exhibit a positive patronage of religion and morality; . . . [and] c) restrict by juridical processes the spread of opinions, and . . . external actions that tend to destroy in the community belief in God and fidelity to moral standards.[18]

This final duty, he claimed, is to be "regulated by the norms of political prudence, which may dictate toleration of errors and evils affecting the social order, when and insofar as such toleration is demanded by the common good, or required lest greater evils result."[19]

Without employing the language of the "*thesis/hypothesis*" distinction, Murray appears here to have duplicated nearly exactly the theory of those theologians who were to become his antagonists in the following decade. All of the essential ingredients of their theory are present in this ethical argument: 1) recognition of the duty to worship God as God wills to be worshipped (presumably as taught by the Catholic Church); 2) recognition of the right to act according to the dictates of the moral law and the denial of the right to act according to an erroneous interpretation of this law; 3) establishment of public religion where possible and acceptance of religious toleration only where necessary; and 4) resignation to the probable impossibility of establishing a "Kingdom of God" in a temporal world burdened by the religious division of the human community. Murray seems thus to have arrived "at precisely the conclusion he initially sought to avoid."[20] Although he indicated that in a future article he intended to demonstrate the theological and political bases of the concept of religious liberty, "the sequel never appeared . . . [because] Murray saw that the logic of his thought would lead, with relatively insignificant differences, to the same conclusions as those of the conservative Catholic view."[21]

There are a number of explanations which account for Murray's abandoning this initial schema for his defense of religious liberty. First, Murray's conceptualization of the mediation between the human person and the natural and human laws was either a) too abstract if the individual is supposed to formulate meaningful prudential judgements in complex circumstances guided only by general principles; or b) too institutionalized and impersonal if one considers *only* the Church and the state to be competent in the determination of the content of subjective moral norms.[22]

Murray also abandoned this position because it led to a conclusion which he initially sought to avoid. Namely, it led to the conclusion that there exists no public right to dissent from the truth about God or to worship in a manner other than that prescribed by the Catholic Church. From the point of view of the American Catholic, this would preclude the idea of religious toleration and place the Protestant on the same ethical ground as the atheist. This conclusion was obviously unacceptable in light of Murray's own pre-determined objective.[23]

Murray also abandoned his initial religious freedom argument because of problems inherent in his description of the bifurcated individual/social existence of the human person. For example, if "conscience" is to mediate between objective law and subjective norms, then Murray needed to develop a theory of social reasoning and public rationality to complement his notion of conscience as "a practical judgement of reason by which *a* man judges the morality of a concrete act." Likewise, Murray's concept of "necessary" institutions was problematic because unless he expanded his ethical universe to grant voluntary associations a legitimate role in the formation of right consciences, the state (by virtue of its role in establishing human law) would possess exclusive authority to promote "the collective moral awareness of society."

He also failed to maintain a consistent analogy between the prudential nature of individual and social judgements. Murray seems to have emphasized the permanency and principled quality of personal moral judgements while simultaneously consigning collective political judgements to the realm of the historically conditioned. Thus, the virtue of prudence appears to operate in a manner indicative of a bifurcated experience of individual/social existence.

Finally, the social nature of Murray's own religious beliefs forced him to abandon his initial argument for religious liberty. The ethical universe he described left no room for a public role for religion in the formation of an ethical consensus based on principles of reason alone. Again, only the individual and the state were capable of mediating universal principles in historical circumstances. Such a position was clearly incompatible with the social nature of the Catholic faith.[24]

These liabilities of Murray's initial defense of religious liberty need not obscure its contributions to an understanding of Catholic teaching on the subject. First, he indicated that a distinction of the ethical, theological, and political dimensions of the problem was necessary for intelligent discussion of the issue. He also recognized that one might reasonably expect to achieve an initial consensus only by remaining on the level of ethical principle. Finally, he began to develop his appreciation for the distinct (but not separate) and complex (but not confused) configuration of orders and institutions which contribute to the individual and social experience of the moral life of the human person.[25]

The dialectical quality of Murray's thought will become more apparent as we now examine how he developed these valuable insights and corrected his conceptual problems in the next phase of his defense of the principle of religious liberty.

The Historical Series (1948-1950)

After failing to produce an adequate theory of religious liberty on the basis of an abstract ethical argument, Murray began a study of the history of the effort to establish an appropriate relationship between the institutions and imperatives of the spiritual and temporal societies. He acknowledged that his investigation henceforth "must proceed from an historical point of view [because] nothing is more unhelpful than an abstract starting point,"[26] and in this way he began the critical evaluation of the efforts of both medieval and modern theorists which we considered in Chapters 1 and 2.

In Chapter 1, I outlined Murray's argument in defense of John of Paris' appropriation of the principles of social dualism within the context of the thirteenth century political struggle between Boniface VIII and Philip the Fair. In Chapter 2, I described Murray's critique of Robert Bellarmine's interpretation of the principles of social dualism within the context of the post-Reformation political environment, and I also noted that while Murray regarded Leo XIII as a faithful witness to this ancient tradition in his nineteenth century statement of the *principles* of the Gelasian Thesis, he also recognized the need to separate principle from polemic in Leo XIII's *application* of these principles. These chapters should suffice as a demonstration of Murray's work as a student of the history of political theory. It therefore remains for us to consider the nature of the *theoretical* advances Murray made in this stage of his defense of religious liberty. Two particular theoretical advances stand out as significant milestones during this period.

First, Murray appears to have recognized the need to emphasize the qualitative distinction that exists between natural and human law. Like Aquinas, Murray insisted that "the natural law is altogether unchangeable in its first principles." On the other hand (also like Thomas), he recognized that the human law "can be rightly changed on account of the changed condition of man to whom different things are expedient according to the differences of his condition."[27]

He further emphasized that the abstract principles of the natural law did not find an immediate place in the constitutional law of a particular country. Human law represents the mediation of these abstract principles within "the juridical exigences created by a situation of political fact."[28] One may rightly argue that this distinction complicated the issue with which Murray grappled. However, this distinction was also completely necessary in order to demonstrate that human social existence could be (and in fact is) complex without being confused.

After recognizing the contingency of the human law, Murray began to explore the nature of a rational political regime. He considered the rational political regime (or the "adult" or "mature" state) to be that in which "the means for its self-direction to right spiritual and moral ends exist within the political order itself." This is not to say that the state provides the means whereby human persons achieve their ultimate end in the spiritual realm. Rather, the state exists to secure the conditions of freedom requisite for all individuals to achieve the actualization of their potentialities as spiritual and political beings. The "adult" or "mature" state (the rational political regime) is therefore one in which "the political mood is the mood of freedom" and in which all recognize that "freedom is the citizen's highest right, that freedom is the highest political end, and that the function of the state itself . . . is the ordering of freedoms into an *ordo legalis*."[29]

In a rational political regime, the power of the state would exist primarily to preserve the freedom of individuals and institutions within society. As an institution within society, the Church would enjoy the freedom necessary to fulfill her spiritual mission of worshipping God and teaching its doctrine without interference from the state.

Murray believed that many times in the course of history either the Church had extended its power beyond the realm of the spiritual or the state had attempted to diminish the legitimate freedom of the Church. Many theorists had either over-estimated or under-estimated the legitimate authority and power of the Church in its relationship to the state. For example, in the nineteenth century, Leo XIII believed that laicist states (whose constitutions espoused the secularist principles of continental liberalism) were denying the legitimate freedom of the Church. Leo therefore condemned the separation of Church and state without recognizing that a *lay* (as opposed to a *laicist*) state might best serve the needs of the Church by defending the freedom of all through a system of democratic institutions.

Murray proposed a statement of Catholic doctrine that incorporated these complementary notions of the contingency of human law and the idea of the "mature" state. If such institutions as religious establishment and legal intolerance, for example, were indeed principles of human law and necessary only in a state incapable of ordering freedom to protect the basic liberties of its citizens, then they did not exist with the same doctrinal status as the abstract principles of natural law. He could thus advance to the next stage in the development of his theory of religious liberty by noting that *only* "'freedom of the Church' . . . is inherently demanded by the Gelasian Thesis." He challenged his contemporaries to recognize that Catholic Church-state theory does not include as a matter of *principle*, the concepts of the "religion of the state" or legal intolerance.[30]

The Catholic University Series (1951-1952)[31]

By locating the institutions of establishment and intolerance within the sphere of the historically-contingent, Murray struck the first

blow at the Church-state theory of his contemporaries. He thus initi-
ated a bombastic polemical exchange which often included *ad homi-
nem* vitriol. In the course of this debate, Murray criticized the attempt
to establish the concept of "the religion of the state" as a permanent
feature of Catholic Church-state theory. In repudiating the transtemporal value of this concept, he began to develop a sociological nomenclature which included the society/state distinction. This distinction would later form an essential element of his final defense of religious liberty. In this stage of his career, Murray also began to develop
a notion of "the people" which was necessary to correct the defects
inherent in his concept of social reasoning and collective rationality.

Murray fired the opening salvo in this controversy in his articles
analyzing the historical application of the Gelasian Thesis. George W.
Shea responded to Murray's rejection of the transtemporal value of the
concept of the religion of the state by noting that Murray himself had
advanced a theory which obliged the state to acknowledge God as its
author and to worship Him as He wills to be worshipped.[32] Shea then
re-iterated his argument that "in a Catholic society . . . the formal,
official, and exclusive recognition and profession of Catholicism by
the state as its one and only religion . . . seems necessarily contained
in the very notion of the state's duty to profess the true religion."
This "official and exclusive recognition and profession" of the Catholic faith designated Catholicism as "the religion of the state."[33]

Murray responded with a full-length rejoinder to Shea's reply.[34]
Initially, he set out what he considered the broad outline of his own
theory of Church-state relations. He argued that the first elements of
any Church-state theory must be the principles of social dualism which
comprise what we have termed the Gelasian Thesis. These principles
further imply the necessity of preserving the freedom of the Church,
the personal integrity of the individual, and harmony or *concordia* between the spiritual and temporal societies. At this point, Murray distinguished the terms civil society, political society, state, and government[35] and insisted on the recognition of the circumscribed role of the
state in the life of the temporal society.[36]

Turning from these abstract principles, Murray confronted the
problem of their application in particular historical circumstances.
Here he recognized that "by their embodiment in institutions, the prin-

ciples, without ceasing to be transtemporal as principles, become temporal as applications of principles." He believed that the Church in the twentieth century faced the prospect of "changing applications of principles" as a result of "the changing character of 'the state'" and its gradual "maturation." Further, the Church needed to recognize that "the legal institution known as the state-church . . . [and] the concept of Catholicism as 'the religion of the state' represent[ed] an application . . . [but not a] permanent and unalterable exigence of Catholic principles."[37]

The Church in the twentieth century faced the immediate prospect of adapting to the changing political circumstances created by the emergence of the democratic state as a rational political regime. It was apparent to Murray that this constitutional arrangement represented "man's best and possibly last hope of human freedom," and it also "offer[ed] the Church as good a hope of freedom as she ever had."[38] The "theological task of the moment" transcended the continuation of endless polemic against the continental liberal form of separation of Church and state. Instead, Murray challenged Catholics in the twentieth century "to explore . . . the possibilities of a vital adaptation of Church-state doctrine to the constitutional structure, the political institutions, and the ethos of freedom characteristic of the democratic state." Specifically, he longed to see the Church apply its "vital law of continual adaptation" to "the provision guaranteeing 'the free exercise of religion' that ha[d] become characteristic of the democratic state constitution."[39]

Murray had thrown down a challenge to which his adversaries would soon respond. He had questioned the doctrinal status and normative value of the concept of "the religion of the state." In characterizing this institution as an historically contingent element of human law, he had also questioned and actually denied the possibility of realizing an ideal relationship between Church and state within any particular historical period. This represented a frontal assault on the time-honored[40] *thesis/hypothesis* distinction and placed Murray, in the eyes of many, well beyond the bounds of orthodoxy in his theological investigations.

Francis J. Connell responded to Murray's challenge to the "manualist" theory of Church-state relations by steadfastly maintaining the orthodoxy of the argument in defense of the normative value of establishment and intolerance.[41] He wrote that Catholic doctrine ascribed to civil rulers both the "obligation to obey the positive law of our Savior in their official acts" and the "right to restrain non-Catholic propaganda and proselytizing."[42] In his mind, there was no need to seek any further development in Catholic teaching on this subject, nor ought one attempt to defend the idea of religious liberty because "the traditional ideas of the relationship between Church and state provide[d] all that [was] necessary to give assurance to fair-minded people that the Catholic Church constitutes no menace to the cherished spirit of liberty" so dear to the American people.[43]

Murray did not share this perception of non-Catholic confidence in the Catholic theory of establishment and intolerance. He continued his critique of the concept of "the religion of the state" by demonstrating its incompatibility with the principles of social dualism. It is a matter of principle, he wrote, that "the state is not empowered either to permit or to prohibit the preaching of the Gospel. Nor is the Church in the slightest degree required to go to men through their civil rulers."[44]

Connell's theory was also defective because it was suitable only to a regime governed by an absolute monarch. In any other form of government in which "there is a dispersion of political responsibility and power among a variety of institutions and men," the investigation of the Catholic faith necessary for its meaningful profession would be at best a practical and at worst a conceptual impossibility. Connell's theory of a constitutionally-mandated religion of the state experienced its tragic demise by tending to the inevitable conclusion that it was either incapable of implementation or that it denied "the transcendence of the Church to political forms."

While Murray's rejoinder primarily (and almost exclusively) took the form of a rebuttal, it did presuppose a familiarity with certain definitions which were essential to establish the contingent nature of the concept of the religion of the state. His argument regarding the incompetency of the state to "authorize" or sanction the principles of faith or the activity of worship maintained the distinction between the sacred and secular societies and also implied a limited and circumscribed role for the state within the larger realm of "society." Not only is the state totally incompetent to exercise an authoritative role in the spiritual society, but it is also only a small part of the "patterned ensemble of purposive human associations" which constitute the temporal society.[45] Murray's society/state distinction thus formed an important basis for his criticism of the use of the term "the religion of the state."

His development of a refined concept of "the people" also enabled Murray to dismiss the transtemporal value of the concept of "the religion of the state." Within this term, "the people," Murray included

> both rulers and ruled and their political relationship, the whole contingent order of organized human associations, the total institutionalization, also contingent, of public, private, and group life, and the individual genius that is always stamped upon every genuine people.[46]

Such a social configuration exhibited a diversity which precluded any pretense of religious homogeneity and therefore described a political entity for which the concept of "the religion of the state" was totally irrelevant. Murray would further clarify these definitions of society and state and "the people," but at this stage in the development of his argument for religious liberty they enabled him to dismantle the theoretical edifice which recognized the normative value of establishment and intolerance.

Murray's antagonists responded to his challenge with a restatement of their argument that did not address his understanding of the society/state distinction or the term "the people." Connell responded to Murray's first charge that state investigation and profession of the Catholic faith would be impossible in any regime other than an absolute monarchy by distinguishing between the manner of an official and a private religious act. The state (in whatever form it assumes) fulfills this obligation simply by guaranteeing the full freedom of the Church. The individual, on the other hand, can only fulfill this obligation by embracing the religion taught by the Catholic Church. This distinction, he believed, adequately addressed Murray's concern regarding the conceptual problem of public profession of the Catholic faith.[47]

Connell also disputed Murray's contention that religious liberty represented the most appropriate means for ordering the relationship between Church and state in the democratic societies which existed in the twentieth century. Although he granted the expediency of religious toleration in the United States, Connell insisted that this pragmatic arrangement of institutions did not represent the "ideal" or Catholic *thesis*, nor did it diminish "the obligation *per se* of the government in a democracy such as ours to find out the true religion and to favor it."[48]

Connell seemed to be desirous of some consensus with Murray when he wrote that "the *concordia* of which [he] speaks in the end is indeed a goal to be sought. [And] from the standpoint of the practical ways of attaining this objective I presume we are in substantial agreement."[49] However, Connell insisted on the need to maintain the permanent validity of the argument that in theory, and in the ideal world of the Catholic *thesis*, the state would only fulfill its obligation to recognize and embrace the moral principles of the divine law by establishing the Catholic Church as the religion of the state.

In the end, there could be no reconciliation between Murray and his interlocutors because Murray was certain that his adversaries' theory required an "immediate illation from the order of ethical and theological truth to the order of constitutional law . . . [which was] in principle, dialectically inadmissable."[50]

The Leonine Series (1952-1956)

In his further analysis of the teaching of Leo XIII, Murray discovered that the distinction between "society" and "state" was not only fundamental to any statement of Catholic political theology but also notably denied in the philosophy of continental liberalism. He then continued his argument in defense of religious liberty by contrasting the relationship of society and state in the continental and American political systems in order to distinguish the meaning of religious freedom in these two contexts.

In the first article of his Leonine series, Murray described the totalitarian democracy which was the target of Leo's polemic.[51] He devoted the entire article to a description of this enemy and to a re-iteration of the principles of social dualism. The enemy, those continental states which espoused the political ideals of the Jacobins (whom he labeled the "political heirs of the *philosophes*"), implemented a political philosophy in which the state "identifie[d] itself with society and pretend[ed] to be the highest, indeed the sole, social form of human existence." Such a state was an "apostate state" dedicated to "effecting by political means the apostasy of traditionally Catholic society from belief in God and Christianity." Such an apostasy was the logical conclusion of its philosophy which "asserts the absolute autonomy of the individual human reason" and the moral norm that "man is bound only to obey himself."[52]

Murray continued his analysis of the Leonine texts by examining Leo's understanding of the nature of the struggle between Church and state.[53] He noted that in his condemnation of the separation of Church and state, Leo directed his criticism particularly against the ideological secularism of the "sects." The conflict between the Church and the sects concerned first of all "the order of reality itself—the nature of truth, the norm of morality, the scope of reason, the meaning of freedom, and the mutual relations of freedom and authority, liberty and law." On a second level, the conflict concerned the structure of politics and opposed the sectarian "monism of law and social power" to the Church's understanding of "the dual order of authorities, laws, and societies, and . . . their hierarchy." Finally, the conflict was itself substantive and displayed a laicist political ideology contending against the Christian faith for recognition as "the animating substance of social institutions."[54]

Murray continued to probe Leo's writings for further indications of the truly critical distinction between society and state. He recognized that this distinction was "rather foreign to the later absolutist Continental tradition . . . [and] therefore foreign to the experience of the Papacy which by the time of Leo XIII had been standing within the absolutist tradition for nearly 400 years." He did promise, however, to provide "a separate and extended discussion" of this important issue in a later article.[55]

Murray made good on this promise by contrasting the American and continental political traditions in order to indicate the nature of the society/state distinction. Whereas "the traditional structure of politics had been marked by a distinction of society and state," he wrote, "royal absolutism reversed this situation" and created conditions con-

ducive to allowing the state to draw "the whole of society, including
the Church . . . inside the growing state and . . . the developing arma-
ture of civil law." In such an undifferentiated society-state, "the state-
aspect—the aspect of power and law—increasingly assumed the primacy over the society-aspect, the aspect of culture, education, associa-
tional life (including marriage and the family), and even religious
life." Murray shared Leo's opinion that "totalitarian democracy represented the end-form of this lengthy corruption of traditional political
principle."[56]

By contrast, in establishing their constitutional system, the
American people maintained "the distinction between society and state
and the principle of a government of limited powers." They therefore
"repudiated the Continental concept of the omnicompetent society-
state." Under the American constitutional system, "the state remains
interior to society. . . . [It] is an aspect of society . . . [which] stands in
the service of society and is subordinate to its purposes." In the
United States, "the state is not primatial; society possesses the primacy
over the state." Therefore, to the degree that the spiritual order operates autonomously in society, apart from the control of the state, "the
principle of the primacy of the spiritual over the political holds
sway."[57]

Murray concluded his comparison of the structure of politics
which emerged from the American and the continental political traditions by claiming that their differentiation extended from the theoretical level to the practical manner by which each institutionalized the
separation of Church and state. Separation within the continental tradition represented a form of consent to the Church's

infeudation to an inherently totalitarianizing regime; it would
mean [the Church's] capture within the iron cage of a juridical
and political monism; [and] it would mean the acknowledge-
ment that the state has the power to enfranchise the Church.[58]

On the other hand, separation in the United States recognized
that

the Church is free to be whatever she is [and] the law does not
presume to make any declarations about her nature, nor does
she owe her existence within society to any legal statute.[59]

Thus, after considering Leo's condemnation of the separation of Church and state as it existed in Europe, Murray concluded that "there is still room for an unprejudiced examination of the American concept of separation because this latter concept is different in point of political principle from the concept condemned." This distinction between forms of separation is legitimate because the "'separate state' of the American formula is not in any recognizable sense the 'separate society-state' of the Continental formula."[60] The distinction between society and state therefore differentiates the two manners of separation and so becomes central to an analysis of the normative value of religious liberty.

It was on the basis of the continental liberals' formation of the omnicompetent society-state that Leo condemned the separation of Church and state as an unfathomable infringement on the essential freedom of the Church. Murray indicated, however, that Leo only condemned the separation of Church and state as he witnessed it in nineteenth century Europe.

In the continental liberal tradition, society and state were coextensive whereas in the American political tradition the state possessed only a limited grant of power and remained subordinate to the whole of the temporal society. If it is possible to conceive of two different modes of society-state relations, it must also be possible to distinguish two different modes of Church-state relations. A re-examination of the normative value of the American understanding of the separation of Church and state was therefore possible, especially if it is true (as Murray claimed) that "Leo XIII . . . subordinated the problem of Church and state in the narrow juridical sense to the problem of the Church and human society in the broadest sense."[61] It thus appears that if the Christian structure of politics obtains in a given society, and the state wields only that limited power necessary for the maintenance of public order, then the institution of religious freedom as a juridical concept might not only be tolerable but also possibly a moral imperative.

This refinement of the society/state distinction proved to be a significant milestone in the development of Murray's theory of religious liberty. He applied the concept of the circumscribed function of the state to the problem of governmental care of religion. He noted for example, that government may exercise only a strictly political role in the socio-economic realms of society because it exists on the same plane as these institutions as a constituent element of society.[62] Even where he developed a paternalistic concept of government (as in the case of governmental care of the order of culture or the order of religion), he argued that such state activity was legitimate only in the extreme case in which the use of coercive force was necessary for the preservation of public order in the face of a direct threat to the survival of the moral bases of society.[63]

This precision in his definition of the complexity of the ethical universe allowed Murray to clarify further the manner in which universal principles are meditated to the concrete imperatives of human constitutional law. The theoretical sophistication of his argument overwhelmed any effort to refute his re-structuring of Catholic teaching regarding Church-state relations. As Murray steadily refined his understanding of the theological, philosophical, and political principles which would establish the normative value of religious liberty, his opponents could only resort to the power of ecclesiastical sanctions to prevent the demise of their teaching.[64] These theologians successfully marshalled the ecclesiastical power at their disposal to force Murray to withhold publication of significant articles in which he advanced the development of his defense of religious liberty in the late 1950s. Despite these obstacles to the dissemination of his ideas, however, the authoritative quality of his challenge was becoming ever more apparent.

The Social Monism Argument (1954-1957)

Murray next began a thorough examination of the implications of the Gelasian Thesis as they applied specifically to the *thesis/hypothesis* distinction. As he continued to develop his defense of religious freedom, he argued that, if ever realized in practice, a union of Church and state might itself violate the principles of Christian constitutionalism, and so he saw his "new thinking" as an attempt to avoid the promotion of social monism by the Church herself.

Murray concluded that the failure to recognize and respect the principles of social dualism had historically been the greatest obstacle to the effort to establish an appropriate relationship between the spiritual and temporal societies as well as between the Church and the state. He believed this was also true in the middle of the twentieth century, and so there needed to be a new manner of stating Catholic teaching regarding Church-state relations other than the *thesis/hypothesis* distinction.

Murray admitted that this distinction did have great merit at the time of its inception. ("It registered the Church's opposition to the new 'Liberal state' in its concrete theory, dynamism, and actual religious and social effects.") In the twentieth century, however, it labored under the burden of its limited applicability to contemporary historical circumstances. At a minimum, its principles were not universally valid. Indeed, they appeared to overlook the benefits enjoyed by the Church in "the greatest, fundamentally most sound, and historically most fruitful political experiment of modern times, the United States of America."[65]

The *thesis/hypothesis* distinction was also problematic because in its conclusions it tended to blur the necessary distinction of the spiritual and temporal societies which the principles of social dualism required. Specifically, "the *thesis* could not fail to imply some espousal of [Church] authority in political affairs," and likewise "the *hypothesis* could not fail to imply some rejection of the method of freedom." It thus appeared that the *thesis/hypothesis* distinction tended to a "diminution of the cardinal principle that is the heart of the ancient Gelasian doctrine, [i.e.] the freedom of the Church and her transcendence to all political forms."[66]

A re-thinking of Church-state theory in the twentieth century was also necessary because "the old situation in which the idea of right order was endangered by a false theory of freedom . . . [gave] way to a new situation in which the true idea of freedom [was] endangered by a false theory of order."[67] That is, the social monism fostered by the totalitarian democracy of continental liberalism was no longer a threat to the freedom of the Church. Instead, twentieth century society confronted a social monism engendered by the totalitarian communism of Marxism-Leninism.

Murray believed that in order to meet the new challenge to the principles of social dualism, the Church should respond with the best means available in the historical circumstances of the twentieth century. Specifically, the Church ought to foster the growth of national communities' emerging consciousness of their constitution as a "people." The Church would best promote the application of the ancient principles of the Gelasian Thesis by continuing Leo XIII's project of shifting "the terms of the major problem from the limited ones, 'Church and state,' to the broader one, 'Church and human society.'"[68] In an age in which peoples were becoming ever more conscious of their immunities from the power of government, the Church would best secure its own freedom by directly enlisting the support of whole societies which exude the spirit of liberty so characteristic of a democratic age.

A people's consciousness of their freedom in a democratic society is a sign of its political maturity and its need to transcend the authoritarian structures which grant official state support to particular statements of religious truth and values. This consciousness of freedom, which characterized the constitutional democracies which emerged from the Anglo-Saxon tradition, indicated an advance beyond the historical moment in which Church-state relations were best ordered within the context of the *thesis/hypothesis* distinction. If the Church was to counter effectively the totalitarianism of communism, it would have to challenge society in a manner befitting its political maturity. The Church must therefore come to a new understanding of its proper "relation" to the state.

This idea of "relation" is appropriate only to the "order of action." It is not "constitutive of the being" of the Church, the state, or something distinct from both. The character of such "relations" is perpetually changing. What was (and always is) necessary, therefore, is a theological investigation of Church-state relations which distinguishes "the permanent purposes of the Church in her relations to the state from the contingent means of achieving these purposes."[69] Murray believed that the Catholic Church should seek the institutionalization of its transtemporal principles within a democratic society if it were to challenge effectively the twentieth century form of social monism—communist totalitarianism.

In order to accomplish this re-structuring of Church-state relations, theologians would have to transcend the historically conditioned confines of the *thesis/hypothesis* distinction. Murray located Papal approval of such new thinking in Pius XII's address *Ci riesce.*[70] Although his opponents disputed his interpretation of this address,[71] Murray argued that Pius XII had intended it to represent a moment in doctrinal development on the question of Church-state relations. In an address at Catholic University, Murray argued that Pius XII had questioned the following aspects of the *thesis/hypothesis* distinction: 1) its narrow conception of the problem; 2) its defective method; 3) its failure to recognize all relevant principles of Catholic doctrine; and 4) its faulty construction of the Catholic tradition.[72]

Murray first claimed papal approval for his contention that the *thesis/hypothesis* distinction applied only in the historical context in which the national sovereign-state was the predominant form of political organization. He believed that Pius XII had challenged theologians and jurists to consider the situation of the universal Church as it confronts a politically diverse international community in the twentieth century. In this new framework of Church-state relations, the needs of the universal Church and the international community must take precedence over the needs of local churches and particular states.[73]

Murray also claimed Pius' support for his rejection of the almost exclusively juridical method employed by proponents of the *thesis/hypothesis* distinction. He believed that Pius XII had promoted a more complex pattern of normative values, and he noted that Pius had insisted that all discussion of Church-state relations and any doctrinal development on this issue must be informed by a people's sense of history—particularly its political history. Murray further claimed the approbation of Pius XII for his contention that there must be mediating factors between the realm of the abstract and the particular, for Pius' assertion of the primacy of theological and ethical principle over positive law was also accompanied by a recognition of the fact that the abstract principles of theology and ethics require the mediating influence of the science and art of jurisprudence if they are to be embodied in the constitutional and statutory law of a particular state.[74]

Murray concluded that Pius XII himself was a critic of the *thesis/hypothesis* distinction because of its failure to embody true principles of Catholic theology and its faulty construction of the Catholic tradition. Pius XII rejected the unconditional absoluteness of the exclusive rights of truth and the negation of all rights of error. He rejected the idea that the right to repress error is inherent in government. Finally, he denied the notion that the mere possibility of intolerance justified its application in particular circumstances.[75]

According to Murray, Pius XII believed that the highest controlling principle of the juridical order was the concept of the common good (understood as the unity of a people and the establishment and maintenance of the public peace). The ultimate criterion in determining Church-state relations within the concrete exigences of constitutional law was therefore the utility of a particular legal arrangement for the promotion of the common good. By implication, then, neither establishment nor non-establishment, neither intolerance nor toleration are constituent elements of a "Catholic *thesis*." None of these social arrangements exists *a priori* as an element of Catholic dogma. All represent historically contingent socio-political arrangements whose institutionalization depends exclusively on their utility for the promotion of the public good, and all are therefore elements of a *hypothesis* situation (although this label is itself misleading given the impossibility of achieving an "ideal" relationship between Church and state).[76]

Murray considered Pius XII's *Ci riesce* address to be a vindication of his own theological investigation into the doctrinal status of the *thesis/hypothesis* distinction. He believed that theologians would now recognize the polemical nature of Leo XIII's condemnation of the separation of Church and state and begin to read his encyclicals in the light of Pius XII's contribution to the Catholic understanding of the Gelasian Thesis. Murray believed that unless Catholics transcended the time-bound strictures of the *thesis/hypothesis* distinction, they would be guilty of promoting a form of "Catholic Jacobinism" which held that those who would not profess the Catholic faith were not a part of the state in the so-called "Catholic nations."[77]

With this last articulation of the need for a re-statement of the authentic principles of social dualism, Murray reached the point at which he could finally synthesize his ideas into a systematic statement of the normative value of religious liberty. He had distinguished universal abstract principles from their historically-contingent applications. He had refined his notion of "the people" and his distinction between society and state in his rejection of the doctrinal status of the concept of "the religion of the state." Finally, he had stated the value of political prudence as the means for mediating theological and ethical principles in constitutional and statutory law.

It is probably true that the conclusions expressed in these works led to the censorship of Murray's writings in the late 1950s. One could not deny, however, that by this point he had laid a stable foundation for his argument that the legislation of a constitutionally-guaranteed right to religious liberty represented the most appropriate manner of ordering Church-state relations in the twentieth century.

Interim Arguments (1958-1960)

It was in the midst of the tumult which accompanied the conflict between Murray and his antagonists that he produced some of the most lucid arguments in defense of his theory of religious liberty. During this period, Murray submitted two articles[78] to censors in Rome. Bowing to the objections of his superiors, he published neither. Any study of the development of Murray's political thought must include an examination of these works, however, for they represent the debut of his synthesis of the various conceptual elements which were emerging as the fruit of his now decade-long study of the problem of religious freedom.

In these articles Murray clearly delineated the distinction between his own argument and those of opponents. Noting at the outset that all Catholics agree that the principles of Christian constitutionalism assume that there are two societies, two authorities, and two laws, he went on to state that the problem of religious freedom is essentially a problem of establishing a right relationship between these societies, authorities, and laws. Since Catholics also agree that those responsible for the establishment of this right relationship must always secure *libertas ecclesiae* and *concordia*, he concluded that the issue must therefore revolve around the actual character of governmental care of religion.[79]

Governmental care of religion, according to the manuals of public ecclesiastical law, included both legal establishment and intolerance of dissent. Murray noted, however, that establishment and intolerance are *per se* principles of constitutional and statutory law, *not* theological principles. What distinguished Murray from his contemporaries was his solution to the problem of determining "the correct *impostazione* of Catholic doctrine with regard to these two institutions."[80] He therefore organized his analysis of the two solutions to the problem of Church-state relations as a comparison of the "disjunctive" and the "unitary" theories.

The disjunctive theory began with the premise that "the Catholic religion is the one true religion which by divine law ought to be the personal religion of all men and the public religion of all societies of men." It then concluded that "the Catholic religion ought to be 'the religion of the state,' established by human law as the one and only public religion of all political societies, with all the juridical consequences that follow from such a situation of constitutional law."[81] This statement of Catholic doctrine seemed to require the immediate embodiment of theological principle in constitutional law.

When moving from the level of principle to practice, its criterion of application is that of *possibility*. That is, the Catholic Church is to be the religion of the state and the state is to exterminate heresy and error from public life whenever possible (assuming the presence of a Catholic majority in a particular country). This is the Catholic *thesis*.

Where it is not possible to establish the Catholic *thesis*, it is necessary to suspend principle (an act that is evil in itself, but a lesser evil than the disturbance of the public peace) and secure religious toleration—i.e., equal liberty for all religious groups. This, of course, is the *hypothesis*, and its criterion of application is *necessity*. In other words, "toleration is to end as soon as the necessity for it ends and intolerance becomes a possibility."[82]

In the disjunctive theory, legal establishment and intolerance were absolute ideals included within the greater concept of the ideal Christian society; both institutions assumed the status of dogma. This view also recognized any form of separation of Church and state as intrinsically evil while it considered only the union of Church and state and the establishment of Catholicism as the religion of the state to be good.[83]

The unitary theory shared the premise that "religious unity among men, and moral order in individual and social life, are the will of God." This premise included the theological principles that "[1)] there is one true Church to which all men are called; [2)] there is one religious and moral authority to which all men are to give obedience; [and 3)] there is one moral order which governs both personal and social life."[84]

What distinguished the unitary theory from its disjunctive counterpart was its recognition that "religious division and moral incoherence in personal and social life are the human conditions of fact." This human condition of fact is also a theological condition of fact, for the existence of division and incoherence is described in Scripture, and it is also a matter of Catholic doctrine that God tolerates the existence of evil and makes it serve the cause of ultimate good. From this addition to its original premise, the unitary theory reached the conclusion that 1) the suppression of evil is not *per se* good; and 2) the toleration of evil is not *per se* evil. Further, the suppression of evil is not the highest duty of human authority; in fact, there may be circumstances in which the toleration of evil is morally obligatory, and therefore good.[85]

In determining the proper relationship between Church and state, the Church, in fulfilling its *spiritual* and *religious* purpose, must make its theological and moral judgements on the basis of one norm alone: is a given statement or action in accord with objective truth and the consequent obligations of the human conscience to do what is objectively true and good?[86] In promoting "the unity which is peace" (its *political* purpose), however, the state must make its judgements in light of two norms. The first of these is the same moral norm which also controls the judgements of the Church: is a given statement or action in accord with truth and morality? Additionally, the state must also confront its obligation to meet the demands of a juristic norm: is a decision necessary or useful for the public advantage in the given circumstances?[87] These two norms proceed from the understanding of human law as "*disciplina cogens metu poena.*"[88]

In confronting the question of religious liberty, the Church and the state must first consider whether this human law is in harmony with the moral norm which requires respect for the freedom of the

Church and the principles of social dualism. Only then may the state determine whether toleration or intolerance would better promote the public advantage and the common good in a given set of circumstances. Further, in determining the content of human law regarding Church-state relations, statesmen are to consult the competent spiritual authority in order to understand fully the imperatives of the relevant moral norm. However, only statesmen themselves are competent to determine the exigences of the juristic norm, and they possess exclusive authority to make prudential judgements of this sort.[89]

Because the juristic norm does not admit an "ideal" solution that exists *a priori* and independent of particular historical circumstances, the unitary theory does not regard either establishment/intolerance or non-establishment/toleration as dogma or an ideal. The goodness of each depends on its contribution to the public advantage and the common good. It is on this basis that the unitary theory judged as evil the separation of Church and state and the secularization of society which proceeded from the philosophy of continental liberalism and found its codification in laws such as the French Law of Separation of 1903. It is also on this basis that it judged as good that separation and religious freedom which emerged from the tradition of Western constitutionalism and remains preserved in the First Amendment to the U.S. Constitution.[90]

This distinction between the two theories' essential premises and conclusions demonstrated Murray's ability to transcend polemic and view from an Archimedean point the theological debate regarding Church-state relations. In these interim arguments he not only presented both positions dispassionately and in their logical unity, but he also portrayed the superior sophistication of the unitary theory which was clearly his own. His effort to explain the mediation of universal theological and ethical principles in the juridical realm of practical politics appears to have reached a level of maturity that was only possible as a result of the thorough philosophical analysis of the nature of human social existence which had occupied his attention for over ten years.

Though he agonized over his inability to publish these articles, Murray could be confident that his unitary theory was theoretically superior to the disjunctive theory of his antagonists. While he had demonstrated his complete agreement with their statement of the theological premise from which both arguments proceeded, his conclusions indicated that he had come to an even more refined understanding of the implications of that theological premise, for he also accounted for the theological fact of division and evil in the human community and the role of God's toleration of that evil in salvation history. Further, he alone recognized that such historically-contingent institutions as religious establishment, legal intolerance, etc. could only exist in the realm of *praxis*. By their very nature, they could not possibly represent transtemporal elements of the abstract imperatives of the moral order or of Catholic dogma. Although he was not permitted to publish the articles in which he explained these theoretical advances, Murray could rest assured that the truths he had discovered would not remain hidden forever.

Glossary

Christian constitu- the establishment of a political regime which pro-
tionalism: tects and promotes the freedom of the Church and
organizes its institutions in a manner consistent
with the principles of the Gelasian Thesis.

disciplina cogens "an order compelling by fear of a penalty."
metu poena:

Disjunctive explanation of Catholic doctrine regarding Church-
theory: state relations which distinguished between the
thesis and the *hypothesis* and described the ordering of institutional relationships as either "ideal"
or "tolerable," "principled" or "expedient."

Governmental the use of the coercive power of the state to
suppression of eliminate from the public forum ideas and prac-
heresy: tices opposed to those of a constitutionally-
established state religion.

hypothesis: in the political theology of John Courtney
Murray's contemporaries, the acceptance of equal
toleration of all religious groups in a religiously-
pluralistic society in which it is impossible to establish Catholicism as the religion of the state.

Religion of the that system of belief and/or worship which the
state: members of a civil society are constitutionally required to avow or practice.

Religious a constitutional grant of a privileged status to a
establishment: particular religious group within a civil society.

thesis: in the political theology of John Courtney
Murray's contemporaries, the "ideal" political
order in which the Catholic Church would be established as the religion of the state and enjoy the
favor of governmental suppression of heresy.

Unitive theory: explanation of Catholic doctrine regarding Church-
state relations which denied the possibility of an

historical realization of an "ideal" relationship between Church and state and instead insisted that the eternal and immutable principles ordering this relationship must be embodied in institutional arrangements which vary according to different historical circumstances.

Discussion Questions

1. Assess the value of articulating a theology that distinguishes what is "ideal" and what is "tolerable."

2. Is the choice of a "lesser evil" ever to be considered a choice that is good in itself? How, for example, does one choose between candidates for political office when both support policies that one considers immoral?

3. What criteria should the state use to determine when *immoral* behavior ought also to be declared *illegal?*

4. What response would you offer to the assertion of Murray's contemporaries that "error has no rights?"

5. To what extent is the distinction between "society" and "state" respected in the United States? What are the strengths and weaknesses of political ideologies which either seek to limit the power of government or, alternatively, rely on the power of government to solve social problems?

6. Do you foresee human persons organizing themselves in political societies that are more "mature" than those which presently exist? If so, what would be some of the characteristics of such a society? If not, what factors are preventing any further political maturation of society?

7. In your estimation, is the fear of any one religious group imposing its beliefs on society so great that Americans would prefer the erection of an impenetrable "wall" between Church and state to the limited inclusion of specific religious beliefs and practices (e.g., prayer) in the public life of this country?

8. In what ways did the Church transgress the principles of social dualism in theory or in practice from the time of Gelasius I through the middle of the 20th century?

Chapter 4

The Argument for Religious Liberty in its Final Phase

The Conciliar Argument (1963-1965)

As Murray obediently foreswore the publication of the articles which contained his lucid and doctrinally-sound arguments in defense of religious liberty, he also endured his exclusion from participation as a *peritus* (i.e., expert) at the first session of the Second Vatican Council.[1] Without consulting this eminent scholar who had devoted over ten years of study to the question of religious freedom, both the Secretariat for Promoting Christian Unity and the Theological Commission submitted drafts of a statement on religious liberty, but neither of these, nor a compromise draft, won the support necessary for true consensus, and so the first session ended without any substantive discussion of the issue.[2] At this point, Murray received an invitation to come to Rome as a *peritus* from Francis Cardinal Spellman after the latter recognized the necessity of charting a new course in the discussion of religious liberty. Then, during the second session of the Council, the Secretariat's original work on religious liberty (i.e., Chapter V of the Schema on Ecumenism) became a subject of discussion for the Council Fathers.[3]

Murray observed that the Secretariat's treatment of the issue was good as far as it went, but he believed that it did not go far enough to protect and promote religious liberty as a fundamental human freedom. He noted that this text considered religious liberty both as an "immun-

ity of the human person from all coercion in what pertains to his personal relations with God" and as an empowerment for "the free exercise of religion in civil society." It based this freedom on the "right of
nature (*ius naturale*) to the free exercise of religion in society according to the dictates of . . . personal conscience" and on the obligation
of the state and its citizens to "acknowledge this right, to respect it in
practice, and to promote its free exercise."[4]

Despite their good intentions, however, Murray believed that the
authors of this first statement had not produced a satisfactory document. They did not make sufficiently clear the norms which would
sanction the legal limitation of the right of religious freedom. They
might also have improved this document by recognizing and incorporating the traditional principle of "the incompetence of the secular political authority in the field of religion." Murray had hoped that the
statement on religious liberty would have re-affirmed the Church's
commitment to "extend her pastoral solicitude beyond her own boundaries . . . [in order to] assume an active patronage of the freedom of
the human person." Had the Council Fathers incorporated these sug-
gestions, they might have better manifested the Church's nature as "a
tradition of growth in fuller understanding of the truth."[5]

After a series of meetings failed to produce consensus regarding
its final manner of inclusion in the conciliar texts, the Council Fathers
voted to postpone further discussion of the question of religious liberty
until the third session. This postponement of discussion provided
Murray the invaluable opportunity to summarize in an extended article
the currents of thought which contributed to the conciliar debate on
religious liberty.[6] He also used this article to demonstrate again the
superiority of his "unitary" view of the Church-state question as a
basis for the Council's defense of religious liberty.

In a manner very similar to that which he employed in the articles written just prior to the Council, Murray began by distinguishing
the two major positions taken on this issue. In an effort to avoid
needless antagonism, he described these positions simply as the "first
view" and the "second view." The characteristics of the first view
should by now be very familiar—it is "abstract and simple." It affirms the moral principle that "the state is bound not only on the natural law but also on the positive divine law." Its adherents conclude

from this premise that "the state has the duty . . . to recognize by constitutional law that the Church is a perfect society *sui iuris* and that it is the only religious society which has a right *iure divino* to public existence and action." Proponents of this view also demand the recognition of the Catholic Church as the religion of the state and deny to other religions the "legal right to public existence and action in society." This first view thus "affirms the legal institution of intolerance as the logical and juridical consequence of the legal institution of 'establishment,'" and it suffers toleration only in countries in which "the religio-social situation is pluralistic [and] Catholics are . . . a minority."[7]

The "second view" considers the problem of Church-state relations to be "concrete and historical." It therefore begins with an analysis of the "signs of the times" in order to determine the appropriate manner of ordering these relations. In the twentieth century, the decisive factor which affects the question of Church-state relations is "the growth of man's . . . political consciousness." Specifically, peoples have become conscious of the fact that they ought to possess a certain measure of political freedom, "that is, freedom from social or legal restraint, except insofar as these are necessary." This political freedom, the possession of the collectivity known as "the people," serves to protect the freedom of the individual, i.e., the "freedom for responsible personal decision and action in society."[8]

As a result of this growing consciousness of the inalienable right to personal and political freedom, the terms of the Church-state question manifested an altered structure of argument. The Church may no longer state its teaching in terms proper to the medieval, post-Reformation, or even the nineteenth century political environment. The issues of the rights of truth and error, establishment and intolerance no longer hold sway; in the twentieth century, "the terms of the argument . . . [are], quite simply, religious freedom." It therefore remained for the Church to determine "first, what religious freedom means in the common consciousness today, and second, why religious freedom . . . is to receive the authoritative approval of the Church."[9]

Within this second view, there were two schools of thought which attempted to account for the normative value of religious liberty. One group attempted to defend religious freedom "as formally a theological-moral concept which has juridical consequences . . . within the order of constitutional law." Such a justification of religious liberty was vulnerable to the same criticism leveled at the first view, i.e., the objection that it is too abstract and unrealistic in assuming the possibility of an "ideal" instance of constitutional law. This argument also tends to the conclusion that the sincere individual, who may in fact be in error, nevertheless enjoys a degree of freedom to remain in error. Such an argument implies a role for the state in the determination of truth and error. This faculty, however, does not adhere to the state according to the principles of the Gelasian Thesis.[10]

The second school of thought within the "second view" denied the premise that one could address the question of religious freedom solely in terms of "*a priori* [principles] or in the abstract." While the ultimate bases of religious freedom did indeed exist in theological and ethical principles, it is important to recognize that "religious freedom is [also] an aspect of contemporary historical experience."[11]

One may assume that Murray himself espoused the theory he described as the second school within the "second view" because its principles reflected those ideas which he had been clarifying in his works for nearly twenty years. In this view, the concept of religious freedom reflected the contemporary consciousness that such a freedom included immunity from coercive constraint to act against one's conscience as well as immunity from restraint or impediment in acting in accord with the dictates of conscience. In order to arrive at the conclusion that the Church ought to bless this concept of religious liberty, one must construct an argument which incorporates the basic tenets of Murray's political theology.[12]

Assuming the distinction between the sacred and the secular societies, the distinction between society as a whole and the state as a constituent element of that society, the distinction between the concepts of the common good (which is the goal of society) and public order (which is the object of the state's activity), and the wisdom of the dictum "as much freedom as possible, as little constraint and restraint as necessary," one may begin to ground the concept of religious freedom in both theological and ethical principle as well as in sound political policy. On the level of theological and ethical principle, this concept affirms the freedom of the Church as well as the personal and political freedom of the individuals who seek to become fully human by means of their active participation in the life of the spiritual and temporal societies. These are abstract concepts of divine and natural law. For their teaching regarding the normative value of religious freedom to be relevant to contemporary society, however, it remained for the Fathers of the Council to explain its mediation in human law.

In order to mediate the imperatives of the divine and natural law within the contingent realm of human history, the state must recognize the political principle that "the public power is not the judge of religious truth or the secrets of conscience." The public power exists to secure that order necessary for the meaningful exercise of freedom as both immunity and empowerment. Consistent with this understanding of the limited role of the state in the life of society, one may then frame both constitutional and statutory law on the basis of the juridical principle that any legal relationship between Church and state must serve the narrow interests of the public order. In general, the Church and the churches ought to enjoy as much freedom as possible, and experience only as much constraint and restraint as is necessary. States must frame particular laws affecting religion only on the basis of a determination that the jurisprudential criterion of *necessity* requires such action for the preservation of public order.[13]

This argument was Murray's own statement of the normative value of religious liberty. He had hoped that this argument would find a home in the Council's Declaration on Religious Liberty which by the end of the third session had assumed an independent existence. Despite the compelling nature of Murray's statement of the wisdom of this line of argument, however, the Fathers of the Council persisted in their tentative consideration of this issue. Murray summarized their reasons for persevering in their cautious approach to the Declaration on Religious Liberty in another article written during the Council.[14]

He believed the Council Fathers has delayed their approval of the Declaration first, because "in its method and doctrine" the Council was prepared to reject an articulation of the Catholic theory of Church-state relations whose normative value the Church had affirmed since the post-Reformation era. Secondly, there was internal division even among those who sought the Church's support for the principle of religious liberty. There was also a fear that the appearance of ex-

traordinary change in the statement of Catholic doctrine might somehow "cause trouble of conscience or possibly even undermine the authority of the Church" in the minds of some of the faithful.[15]

The most important reason for the postponement of discussion
on the issue of religious liberty, however, was the Church's tardiness
in reading the signs of the times. Murray wrote that "a doctrinal decision on religious freedom was postponed for a year because it had
already been postponed for some two hundred years." In other words,
the Church never went beyond its initial condemnation of the continental liberal form of separation of Church and state in order to consider separation in light of the twentieth century consciousness of the
personal and political freedom of the human person. Theoretical ossi-
fication had set in because the Church failed to recognize this dra-
matic change in the minds of those to whom she ministered. Unless
she quickly recognized the normative value of the principle of religious liberty as it had been "accepted by the common consciousness
of men and civilized nations," the Church ran the risk of "coming to
the battle late, . . . to a war that ha[d] already been won, however
many rear-guard skirmishes remain[ed] to be fought."[16]

Despite the Council's postponement of a vote on the Declaration
on Religious Liberty at the end of its third session, there could be no
turning back. The Declaration was the first order of business as the
fourth and final session opened in September, 1965. The text which
became the subject of debate and revision reflected the principal elements of Murray's own defense of religious liberty with some compromise and concession to the position taken by those Fathers (primarily
the French) who supported the more theologically and ethically-ori-
ented approach.

Murray had to have been pleased by the Council's final text. It
began with the declaration that "everybody has the duty and consequently the right to seek the truth in religious matters . . . [and] pru-
dently form judgements of conscience which are sincere and true."
From this duty and right the Council derived the human person's obligation "to follow this conscience faithfully" in order "to come to God"
who calls all to their final end—eternal life. Given the redemptive
nature of acting according to one's conscience, the Council declared
that the human person "must not be forced to act contrary to his con-

science. Nor must he be prevented from acting according to his conscience, especially in religious matters."[17]

The Council Fathers reflected Murray's influence by citing the incompetence of the civil power in the affairs of the spiritual society as one of the bases of this right. The final text of the Declaration recognized that "the private and public acts of religion by which men direct themselves to God . . . transcend . . . the earthly and temporal order of things." Consequently, "the civil authority, . . . if it presumes to control or restrict religious activity . . . must be said to have exceeded the limits of its power."[18]

The Council approved the text which included these and other statements which bear the mark of Murray's influence on December 7, 1965. Pope Paul VI immediately promulgated the Declaration on Religious Liberty, *Dignitatis Humanae*, and the Church thus finally recognized the normative value of this arrangement of Church-state relations.

Murray quickly noted that the promulgation of this declaration was one of the Council's greatest achievements. It brought the Church "at long last abreast of the consciousness of civilized mankind which had already accepted religious freedom as a principle and as a legal institution." In doing so, it effected a movement from a hierocratic sacralized view of the temporal society to a recognition of its inherent secularity. The Church, he believed, had nothing to fear from such a recognition so long as the principles of social dualism and the freedom of the Church determined the structure of politics.[19]

Murray also noted that this statement of the Church's teaching marked a "transition from the classical mentality to historical consciousness." The Declaration maintained the timeless value of the absolute principles which constitute the Gelasian Thesis, but it also promoted a new and historically relevant application of these principles in the particular context of the twentieth century.[20]

During the years of the Second Vatican Council, Murray witnessed the vindication of his tireless effort to justify the normative value of religious liberty. As a theologian, he served as both critic and facilitator in the effort to justify this novel statement of Catholic doctrine. He ultimately established the credibility of his commitment to the idea of historical consciousness and to the need for constant re-evaluation of the application of universal principles within particular historical circumstances by continuing his investigation of the issue of religious liberty after the Council. As he called for continued reflection on this question, he insisted that his differentiation of the universal and the particular was "not the highest stage in human growth, [for] the movement toward it, now that it has come to term, must be followed by a further movement toward a new synthesis, within which the differentiation will at once subsist, integral and unconfused, and also be transcended in a higher unity."[21]

Moral Agency Arguments (1965-1967)

In the years following the Second Vatican Council, Murray attempted to transcend the distinction of theological, ethical, and political principles. He argued that the contemporary consciousness of the dignity of the human person as autonomous moral agent also required a recognition of religious liberty as a fundamental human right. This marked the final phase of the development of his defense of the normative value of religious liberty.

He believed that those who had approved *Dignitatis Humanae* had based their conclusions on the concept of the *dignity of the human person* rather than on the right of *freedom of conscience*. They had recognized that any statement which considered the rights of conscience always encountered questions regarding the rights of an erroneous conscience or the alleged right of government to repress error. By grounding its understanding of religious liberty on the incompetence of government in religious matters, the Council Fathers avoided these speculative questions and recognized the ability of human persons to understand the objective imperatives of the moral order and to act so as to make those imperatives the subjective norms by which they lived.

Although this change of focus was implicit in *Dignitatis Humanae*, Murray believed that there was still a need to state more explicitly the dignity of the human person as moral agent. He believed that the Declaration did not "develop the idea satisfactorily," nor did it do "more than suggest the line of development to be followed."[22] He wasted little time in taking upon himself the responsibility for developing this line of argument.

The "moral agency" argument for religious liberty "would begin with the traditional truth that every man has the innate dignity of a moral subject." Every human person possesses the intelligence, the self-awareness, and the freedom to make those moral decisions which make life meaningful. These gifts bestow the dignity which distinguishes man from beast, and they also confer a certain amount of responsibility on the human person. Specifically, all people must investigate the objective order of truth and pursue the full realization of their humanity in accord with the objective order of truth. Thus, as a moral agent, the human person "is responsible for the conformity of his judgements of conscience with the imperatives of the transcendent order of truth, and he is responsible for the conformity of his external actions with the inner imperatives of conscience."[23]

Murray distinguished three characteristics of the human person as moral subject (each of which has direct implications for political life). First, in consequence of the human person's innate individuality, all must recognize that while every moral agent pursues the truth in common with others, "the assent to truth is to be personal and free." Second, "the irreplaceability of personal judgement and choice in the moral life" compels all moral agents to act "deliberately and freely" in order to invest their lives with meaning. No external source of meaning may legitimately "substitute itself for the inner dynamisms of intelligence and freedom." Finally, the inviolability of the moral agent's personal integrity "requires that he be surrounded by a zone or sphere of freedom within which he may take upon himself . . . [the] responsibility for his own existence."[24]

Such a description of the nature of the human person as moral agent invests the principle of religious liberty with the character of truth within the structure of the moral universe as Murray has described it. In this moral universe, "inherent in the dignity of man as moral subject is the exigence to act on his own initiative and on his own personal responsibility." This is true "especially in that vital area in which the sense of his own existence, and his pursuit of it, are at stake—that is to say, especially in matters religious." Therefore, the right to liberty in the pursuit of religious truth "is a thing of the objective order . . . rooted in the given reality of man as man. . . . It is identically the basic imperative requirement that man should act in accordance with his nature."[25]

It is with little difficulty that one can derive from this principle the conclusion that "in the juridical order" the human person possesses a "right not to be hindered in acting according to his nature," and consequently a "right to immunity from coercion, especially in matters religious."[26] This is every human person's original claim against all with whom they live in civil society. This claim is particularly significant when directed against the state—that most powerful of all social institutions. While the state itself possesses an original right to preserve public order (a right which is also a matter of moral truth), it may assert the primacy of its right over the right of religious liberty only in the most serious of cases in which the survival of the moral bases of society is in jeopardy. Again, there is to be "as much freedom as possible, and only as much coercion as is necessary."

This "moral agency" argument for religious liberty is completely congruous with Murray's earlier writings on the subject; in fact, it represents the pinnacle of his work on this issue. Assuming, of course, the principles of social dualism, the contingency of human law, and the distinction between society and state, he began by postulating the theological and ethical principle of the dignity of the human person as moral subject. After describing the characteristics of such a moral agent, he then developed the juridical and political principles which would mediate the abstract imperatives of the theological and ethical orders within the concrete circumstances of history.

Specifically, he listed as fundamental juridical principles the axioms that: 1) "the full immunity of the human person from coercion in religious matters is . . . a genuine human right" and 2) "the exercise of the right to religious freedom is to be as free as possible." Corresponding to these juridical principles are the political principles that 1) "government [is] to respect this right and to ensure respect for it in society" and 2) the "legal limitation of the exercise of the right is warranted only by the criterion of necessity."[27]

Just as Murray argued that the human person (individually and collectively) only gradually came to an awareness of the inherent dignity of the moral agent and the consequent right of religious freedom, so I believe that this analysis of the development of Murray's thought reflects his own ever-developing consciousness of the complexity of human social existence and the location of the right to religious liberty within that moral universe. After abandoning the futile effort to establish the immediate application of abstract principles within the contingent realm of history, he pursued an analysis of theological, ethical, juridical, and political principles which revealed the truly complex nature of the problem of religious freedom. Only after he had adequately established the principles of social dualism, the contingency of human law, the society/state distinction, the notion of "the people," the emerging consciousness of the human person, and the dignity of the moral agent could he confidently state the normative value of religious liberty. The fruit of this twenty-two year project, was indeed invaluable, for Murray had finally completed the argument establishing religious liberty as a principle of moral truth within Catholic political theology.

While such an accomplishment represented an end to one aspect of Murray's theological investigations, in other ways, it also represented a beginning. He defended the normative value of a constitutionally-guaranteed right of religious liberty in order to secure the peaceful "coexistence within one political community of groups who held divergent and incompatible views with regard to religious questions." He also realized that once society codified this right, it became necessary to "motivate the general participation of all religious groups, despite their dissensions, in the oneness of the community."[28] By endorsing such a structure of politics, the Declaration on Religious Liberty challenged Murray, and all Catholics, to begin the process of actively contributing to the promotion of the common good while simultaneously retaining their identity as members of a particular religious body.

Discussion Questions

1. How do you evaluate Murray's reaction to the censorship of his writings, the attempt to exclude him from participating in the Second Vatican Council, and his ultimate vindication?

2. Compare the strengths and weaknesses of arguments for religious liberty which locate the basis of such a right in either the autonomy of the individual's conscience or in the incompetence of the state in matters religious.

3. Do you believe that the Church was tardy in reading the "signs of the times" with regard to the question of religious liberty? Is the doctrine articulated in the Declaration on Religious Liberty still relevant to the experience of human persons at the end of the 20th century?

4. Assess the contemporary appreciation of the dignity of the human person as manifested in the laws and customs of this country and throughout the world.

5. Is the value of religious liberty as a fundamental human right universally recognized? If not, what impediments prevent such recognition, and how can they be overcome?

Chapter 5

Religion and Politics in the American Milieu

RELIGIOUS LIBERTY, IN ITS JURIDICAL AND POLITICAL DIMENSIONS, IN-
volves no more than the denial of a privileged status to any particular
religious group and the equal toleration of all. In this sense, religious
liberty aims at no more than the limited objective of securing and
maintaining public peace. Murray, believed, however, that the problem of establishing an appropriate relationship between religion and
politics involves much more than simply the codification of the principle of religious freedom in the constitutional or statutory law of a particular country.

In Murray's political theology, the idea of religious liberty has
consequences far beyond the juridical relationship between Church
and state. In its theological and ethical dimensions, the institution of
religious liberty grants individuals and religious groups not only freedom *from* state coercion in matters religious but also freedom *for* positive action in accord with the dictates of their consciences. By implication, then, this multi-dimensional principle empowers all citizens
to contribute the wisdom of their moral vision to the process of forming a public consensus in a religiously pluralistic society. Without
losing sight of the supernatural end which they ultimately seek, religious people may thus promote the common good which is the naturally ordained and immanently existent *telos* of the temporal society.

Any study of Murray's political theology must therefore transcend the narrowly-defined problem of Church-state relations and con-

sider the broader issue of the relationship of Church and society. Specifically, one must consider his understanding of the Church's role as a moral critic within the complex matrix of institutions that (along with the state) constitute civil society. While the idea of religious liberty obviously precludes the Catholic Church or any other religious or secular community from exercising *exclusive* authority as the conscience of society, one must nevertheless explore the implications of the moral imperative that imposes on religious people and institutions an obligation to participate in the moral life of the temporal society.

In the twentieth century, the Catholic Church presumes the existence of a religiously pluralistic society. It also confronts the difficult task of promoting meaningful and coherent dialogue in such an environment. The formation of a public consensus is only possible if all people share a common language of moral discourse. Murray believed that references to moral imperatives grounded in revealed truths were of limited value in the political life of the temporal society.[1] He concluded that only moral and political reasoning grounded in the tradition of natural law would promote effective political action in a religiously pluralistic society because the dictates of the natural law are rational principles accessible to all reasonable people, whatever their religious persuasion.[2]

True to his commitment to the development of a *practical* political theology, Murray continued to consider the relationship between religion and politics, not simply in the abstract, but also in reference to the actual political life of his own country, the United States. He believed that establishing harmony between the spiritual and temporal societies was not a problem which philosophers and theologians could solve in the abstract or for an "ideal" world. Every citizen of every nation must confront the *practical* problem of appropriately ordering the relationship between the institutions and imperatives of the sacred and secular societies. As an American, it was only logical that Murray sought first to promote this *concordia* in the United States.

Murray thus continued his study of the relationship between religion and politics by investigating the specific relationship between the Catholic Church and American society. He first examined the role of the Church as a moral critic within society, and he specifically urged the Church to speak out against a secularization of society which threatened to exclude the voice of religious groups from all public discourse in this country. He then described the natural law tradition as the best means available to facilitate the formation of a public consensus in this religiously pluralistic nation. Finally, he analyzed concrete political issues which required the immediate attention of American Catholics if society was to make genuine progress toward its ultimate end—the actualization of the human potentialities of its members.

Murray's Critique of "The Secularist Drift"

In addition to affirming the Church's immunity from governmental interference, the Gelasian principle of "the freedom of the Church" also compelled the faithful to exercise a certain degree of moral authority in judging, directing, and correcting the political life of the temporal society. Obviously, the Church could not legitimately claim exclusive authority to exercise this role. She was, however, one of a number of subsidiary institutions with a legitimate interest in the moral life of civil society.

American Catholics were fortunate to live in a country in which there was a benevolent juridical and political relationship between Church and state. Such a situation enabled the Church to speak frankly as a critic of what she perceived to be instances of social injustice. Murray believed that in the twentieth century, the gravest social injustice against which the Church must speak was the ever-increasing tendency to exclude all religious groups from participation in public discourse. The forces promoting the secularization of American society aimed directly at limiting the freedom of the Church and thus struck at one of the fundamental principles of the Gelasian Thesis.

It should not be surprising that Murray located the source of the secularism which he believed to be invading American society in the political philosophy of continental liberalism—particularly in its "political principle of the juridical omnicompetence of the state." This principle allowed the state to declare that it alone "establishes the order of justice and is a law unto itself." The juridical and political consequence of such a philosophy was the absolute separation of

Church and state which Leo XIII and others had condemned. The graver evil, however, was the further attempt "to achieve a completely secularized society in which religion would be denied any vital influence on . . . political, social, economic, or educational life." This political philosophy denied the very existence of the Eternal Law of God as "a higher sovereignty over the . . . authority and action of the state."[3]

While it is true that the U.S. Constitution does not embody the principles of continental liberalism as the political forms of Jacobin democracy did, one must also recognize that American society is not immune to the influence of the secularizing tendencies of this philosophy. Although the Founders of the American regime attended magnificently to "the work of building a City, an order of democratic institutions and culture," they nevertheless "succeeded [only] in erecting an immense structure that encloses . . . a vacuum." In the twentieth century, Americans began to ask "how shall these hollow interstices, within man, within his institutions, be filled?"[4] Murray feared that in this moral vacuum, certain progeny of the philosophy of continental liberalism stood readily available as possible sources of spiritual animation for society.

One form of secularism which threatened to reduce the freedom of the Church to participate in the *res publica* was the myth of "democracy as a religion." This "civil religion" was actually a "secularist faith, created without reference to God or any transcendent law." Its moral and political truths emerged from the will of the majority and were capable of evolutionary (or revolutionary!) revision—no principle could claim universal or eternal validity. Its adherents, comparing the cult of democracy to sectarian Christianity, found in their religion "a more peaceful creed and . . . a higher, more unifying mission . . . [with] more totally salvific resources."[5]

The cult of science represented another form of secularist "religion" which promoted the exclusion of all religious discourse from the political life of the United States. In twentieth century America, the thorough empiricism of the scientific community not only denied the existence of transcendent truths but also regarded as unintelligible any discourse which referred to principles whose proof eluded the language of mathematics and science. This empiricism "narrow[ed] the field of reality and the scope of intelligence." It also "accord[ed] primacy to the material . . . [and] confine[d] all thinking to the categories of the temporal, the quantitative, [and] the relative." Additionally, it "regard[ed] anthropology and psychology as the supreme sciences of man."[6] Finally, it excluded from the public life of society any voice which spoke in an idiom other than that of science. Clearly, then, any religious group whose moral universe included a transcendent referent could find no home in this political environment.

American Catholics could not tolerate the secularization of society which might proceed from the victorious ascendence of either the cult of democracy or the cult of science. These forms of secularism threatened to effect "a certain defacement of the image of God in man." They promoted "a disintegration of rationality [and] a movement of man toward absorption in matter and its processes."[7] Murray considered the total exclusion of transcendent values from political discourse and the total commitment to either the *will* of the majority or to the empirical *facts* of science to be nothing short of "barbarism."

Murray described the "barbarism" of secularism as the failure to organize civil society according to reasonable principles. Though society will never be perfectly rational, its laws and customs ought nevertheless to reflect a certain degree of rationality. Society tends toward barbarism when reasonable social *praxis* yields to the force of one "ism" or another—e.g., majoritarianism, scientism, or even rationalism itself.[8]

Barbarism is also imminent in society when men and women fail to engage in dialogue according to reasonable rules of argument. The threat of barbarism looms when those who participate in the formation of a public consensus employ arguments that are full of passion, pretentious of a form of gnosticism, or insensitive to the value of others' reasonable insights. Barbarism is therefore the human failure to live in community according to the dictates of reason, and the consequent reduction of "all spiritual and moral questions to the test of practical results . . . or to a decision in terms of individual subjective feeling."[9]

In a religiously pluralistic society such as the United States, courage, patience, and humility are necessary in order to repel the barbarism fostered by the ideological progeny of continental liberalism.

American Catholics, and all religious people, need to be courageous in raising their prophetic voices, patient in their inclusion of others' valuable insights, and humble enough to recognize the limitations of their own reason. Because of the fragile quality of a civic unity based on human reason and the reality of irrational elements in human behavior, religiously pluralistic societies always live with the threat of barbarism lurking immediately outside the gates of their City.

The "barbaric" consequences of the spread of secularist ideologies indicated the urgent need to awaken an awareness of the wisdom of the Gelasian Thesis in the minds of Americans. Secularist ideologies, especially the cults of democracy and science, attempted to relegate the Church's activity in the *cura animorum* to the strictly private life of individuals in society. They also attempted to deny the Church access to the *res sacra in temporalibus*. Secularist ideologies failed to recognize that although the family, the employer-employee relationship, and other social relations are not exclusively the concern of either Church or state, they nevertheless fell within the purview of the moral order in which numerous institutions share legitimate authority and set limits to the power of the state.[10]

Murray believed that all religious people in this country ought to recognize that the threat of barbarism is also indicative of the imminence of a contemporary form of social monism. He argued that in their first principles, both the cult of democracy and the cult of science denied the dualistic structure of human social existence. In their political manifestations, both canonized the idea that "it is within the secular state, and by appeal to secular sources, that man is to find the interpretation of his own nature and the means to his own destiny."[11] Such a monist structure of politics would eventually spawn increasingly devastating problems for American society.

Murray argued that all secularist ideologies tend to degenerate into various forms of totalitarianism. He referred to Marxist communism as a concrete example of the secular monism of "political modernity carried to its logical conclusion." He stated that one might trace the roots of this form of social monism to the principles of *conscientia ex lex* and *principatus sine modo sine lege*. More importantly, the history of the oppression which this ideology produced "offer[ed] an empirical demonstration of the fact that there can be no justice where

God is denied and where everything meant by the freedom of the Church is excised from the theorem on which the life of the community is based."[12]

Murray also noted that any attempt to establish a secularist ideology as the animating substance of society would ultimately manifest the *natural* "impotence of the state." The mere existence of this impotence is ironic given the modern state's claim to exclusive moral authority in a temporal society constructed according to the principles of either majoritarian democracy or scientific materialism. One may easily observe, however, that the modern state has proven itself incompetent to provide the *moral* resources necessary to confront numerous social issues. Without the assistance of subsidiary institutions, the state cannot competently address such issues as "crime and civic virtue, education, the stimulation and control of economic processes, public morality, [and] justice in the order and processes of law." Neither the cult of democracy nor the cult of science could overcome such impotence, for they both fail to recognize that "the state depends for its vitality upon a motivation which it cannot itself provide."[13] This motivation must come from other institutions in the complex matrix of civil society.

If the champions of the secularist ideologies were to salvage their political program, their only viable alternative would be to construct the "noble" (or, more accurately, "ignoble") lie that "the whole system of moral values" which constitute the bases of society and provide the means for overcoming the social ills which beset all nations "are now known to be immanent in man." This effort to save their ideologies, however, would not only be "a falsification of history," but more significantly, "a basic betrayal of the existential structure of reality itself." Thus, the problem confronting American society has transcended the issue of the freedom of the Church (which is, of course, a very significant issue in its own right). Quite simply, in twentieth century America, "the issue is . . . truth" and its positive denial by those who would perpetuate the myth of the absolute autonomy of individual reason and the omnicompetence of the state.[14]

Murray proposed that human society in general, and American society in particular, could ultimately choose one of three alternatives as it entered the post-modern age. "On the one hand," he wrote, "post-modern man can continue to pursue the mirage which bemused modern man"[15]—i.e., the claim that the bases of all human rights and liberties are immanent in man and not ultimately derived from the Eternal Law of a transcendent Creator. Such a project could never succeed, however, for the spiritual vacuum which underlies such an illusion would eventually become apparent.

Alternatively, any of a number of immanent ideologies might gain the social power necessary to force their recognition as the animating substance of society. However, once a "non-Christian mode of existence . . . come[s] into being at the heart of human life," it soon "manifest[s] its [own] existence and dynamism," and the consequences of such a revelation are not at all salutary for society. Indeed, even a cursory examination of history demonstrates that "when religious principles cease to govern society, society loses its moral purpose, nations pursue material aims, and the result is war."[16]

One must not despair, however, for "this development into a dreadful chaos of violence in which justice and freedom alike would vanish, is not inevitable."[17] There is an eternal source of wisdom to which post-modern society might turn in order to re-construct a society which recognizes that despite its complexity, human social existence ultimately reflects an inner dynamism which promotes the actualization of the human person's potentialities as both a spiritual and temporal being. By their very nature as rational creatures, all human persons have access to this perennial source of wisdom. With mutual cooperation, it provides the basis for the formation of public peace even in a religiously pluralistic society. Though most often identified with the medieval political and philosophical traditions, its principles are relevant more than ever in the twentieth century. This key to human society's escape from the malaise of modernity was, according to Murray, the "timeless and timely" natural law tradition.

Forging a Public Consensus in the United States

Murray believed that American society was no different from any other in terms of its susceptibility to the forces which promote the secularization of society. As a society, it did not locate the source of its public philosophy within any particular religious or ideological tradition. Its institutional superstructure actually enclosed a spiritual vacuum. There was, however, one difference between the United States and the states of Continental Europe which might mitigate the effects of the "secularist drift." This difference lay in their respective manners of ordering Church-state relations.

Many of the Continental European states codified the philosophical principles of *conscientia ex lex* and *principatus sine modo sine lege* in their constitutional and statutory law. They consequently enforced a separation of Church and state which presumed the power of the state to establish and regulate the public existence of the Church. Such a legal mandate represented a "dogmatic decree that la[id] down a rule of faith." This "dogma" or "faith" proclaimed the principle that "the equality of all religions before God" requires that all religions "be declared equal before the constitutional law of every nation."[18]

The Founders of the American regime never attempted to embody such dogmatic principles in the constitutional law of this country. On the contrary, Murray noted that "the First Amendment is not a piece of religious mysticism, but a practical political principle." This law limited the power of the state to the pursuit of its limited political objective—the public peace of society. It denied the state the power "to legislate [so] as to establish distinctions in citizenship on grounds of religious belief." It also forbade the coercion of "religious conformity as the condition of civic equality."[19] The First Amendment thus safeguarded the freedom of the Church to exercise its proper authority in both the spiritual society and in the *res sacra in temporalibus*.

Murray celebrated the fact that in twentieth century America, all religious groups enjoy a freedom to resist the exclusion of spiritual values from the public life of society. He also recognized, however, that this freedom also imposed a positive obligation on all religious people to overcome whatever obstacles stood in the way of the ecumenical cooperation which was necessary in order to create a structure of politics which reflected the authentic principles of social dualism. He believed that all people of good will should abandon such divisive groups as "Protestants and Other Americans United for Separation of Church and State" and instead form such groups as the hypothetical "Catholics and Protestants and Jews and Other Americans United for

Cooperative Relations Between Church and State in View of the Peril of Secularism, Especially in Education."[20]

Murray described America's religiously pluralistic society as being composed of four distinct "conspiracies."[21] Each of these conspiracies possesses a unique intellectual and historical heritage. The four conspiracies which make the greatest contribution to public life in America are the Catholic, the Protestant, the Jewish, and the secularist. These conspiracies cross paths with one another in a manner that rarely produces true consensus. American society in the twentieth century therefore needed to begin the project of making "the four great conspiracies . . . conspire into one conspiracy that will be American society—civil, just, peaceful, free, one."[22] The realization of this goal would require prodigious effort, and some might argue that it exists more properly in an "ideal" world rather than in the realm of the realistically attainable. At a minimum, however, Murray believed that America's four conspiracies must at least begin the dialogue necessary to keep the forces of "barbarism" outside the gates of the City.

Murray believed that the process of forging an American public consensus must begin with a realistic understanding of the goal of such a consensus. The civic unity to which society might aspire was not a complete unity of mind and heart among all of its members. The social fact of religious division precluded such a goal. Those who would promote the formation of a consensus must therefore appeal to principles which would not "hinder the various religious communities . . . in the maintenance of their own distinct identities." They must guarantee each individual and religious group "the full integrity of their own religious convictions."[23]

The historical experience of American religious pluralism indicated the possibility of establishing a public consensus on the basis of principles understood by reason alone without the assistance of faith. It is a matter of historical fact that in the United States, "political unity and stability . . . [have been] possible without uniformity of religious belief and practice." Likewise, American society stands as a shining example of the fact that "stable political unity . . . can be strengthened by the exclusion of religious differences from the area of concern allotted to government."[24] Murray believed that this *possibility* of forging an effective public consensus consequently established the imperative that Americans must begin to actualize the potential for civic unity.

Murray argued that America's four conspiracies were capable of the cooperation necessary to forge a dynamic public consensus whose "forward-looking historicity" would be "conditioned by the historic past" and also be "the matrix of projects for the future." This consensus would affirm the fact that "there are truths . . . that command the structure and courses of the political-economic system of the United States, . . . [and] We, the People, assent and consent to them." Further, the principles which command the assent characteristic of a public consensus "join harmoniously with other truths in imparting a special character and identity to the American people . . . [who are] a free people democratically organized." Finally, the vitality of the public consensus would be "sustained as it was born, of argument and persuasion, which appeal for their validity to experience and reflective thought."[25]

In order to determine the content of the public consensus, all Americans may consider the wisdom of the ethical imperatives of the natural law. One may participate in fruitful dialogue in this tradition of moral and political reason simply by supposing that "man is intelligent; that reality is intelligible; and that reality, as grasped by intelligence, imposes on the will the obligation that it be obeyed in its demands for action or abstinence."[26] Murray believed that this paucity of prerequisites for participation in political discourse would enable all members of society, theists and atheists, Christians and Jews, Catholics and Protestants, to lend their voices to the formation of a public consensus while simultaneously maintaining the integrity of their most fundamental beliefs about life's ultimate questions.

Murray believed that all members of society would assent to the utility of the natural law tradition in the formation of a public consensus because its presuppositions were self-evident to all reasonable people. He described the systematic nature of this tradition of political reasoning in greater detail, however, in order to demonstrate its value as a public philosophy for American society.

Murray noted that the natural law tradition "supposes a realist epistemology, that asserts the real to be the measure of knowledge, and also asserts the possibility of intelligence reaching the real." The natural law tradition also "supposes a metaphysic of nature" which asserts that "there is a natural inclination in man . . . to achieve the fullness of his own being." It "supposes a natural theology, asserting that there is a God, Who is eternal Reason" and whose creation reflects this rationality. Finally, this philosophical tradition "supposes a morality" which asserts that "for man, . . . the order of nature is not an order of necessity . . . but an order of reason and therefore freedom." Each human person confronts the moral order with the freedom to accept or reject that which will allow one to become more fully human, and so "the moral order is [simply] a prolongation of the metaphysical order into the dimensions of human freedom."[27]

Considered within the context of the natural law tradition, a rationally constructed public consensus ought, at a minimum, to embody "two self-evident principles: '*Suum cuique*,' and the wider principle, 'Justice is to be done and injustice avoided.'" In the application of these principles, "reason particularizes them . . . by determining what is 'one's own' and what is 'just' with the aid of the supreme norm of reference, the rational and social nature of man." In offering examples of the application of these principles, Murray wrote that "their immediate particularizations are the precepts in the 'second Table' of the Decalogue." However, "the totality of such particularizations . . . make up what is called the juridical order, the order of right and justice." In the process of particularizing first principles in the immanent elements of the public consensus, the transcendent principles of the natural law furnish the "moral basis for the positive legislation of the state." They also serve as "a critical norm of the justice of such legislation, and the ideal of justice for the legislator."[28]

Murray believed that one might derive a number of specific principles from the natural law which would prove very familiar to the American people and therefore very relevant to the formation of an American public consensus. Some of these principles have been part of the Western political heritage since the medieval period but are no less relevant to twentieth century American society. Among these principles is the idea of the supremacy of law (law being defined as essentially an act of reason *not* of will). Related to this principle is the location of the source of political authority in the community.

From these principles, reasonable people may also conclude that "the authority of the ruler is limited; its scope is only political, and the whole of human life is not absorbed in the *polis*." Finally, it is possible to derive from these reasonable principles of natural law an understanding of "the contractual nature of the relations between ruler and ruled."[29] All of these medieval principles are not only capable of implementation as part of a twentieth century public consensus but also indicative of the rationality of the Gelasian Thesis with whose principles they are completely compatible.

In their modern and contemporary application, the principles of the natural law provide two additional precepts which might also make a valuable contribution to an American public consensus. The first of these is the principle of subsidiarity. This principle asserts "the right to existence and autonomous functioning . . . [to] various sub-political groups which unite in the organic unity of the state without losing their own identity or suffering infringement of their own ends or having their functions assumed by the state." Like Pius XI and his successors, Murray recognized the beneficence of this principle as a means by which "the freedom of the individual is secured at the interior of institutions intermediate between himself and the state."[30]

The natural law also recognizes the right to "popular sharing in the formation of the collective will" and includes this political principle in the public consensus. Such a principle would win the assent of all reasonable people in American society, for it gives explicit expression to society's recognition of "the dignity of the human person as an active co-participant in the political decisions which concern him."[31]

In most cases, the "principles of action that govern basic human situations . . . are constant and relatively uncomplicated." Where "reason reaches these principles without difficulty," it is likely that there will be little dispute regarding their codification in the constitutional or statutory law of any jurisdiction. One witnesses, for example, the immediate embodiment of natural law principles in the public consensus in the nearly universal existence of some sort of sanctions against "perjury, theft, murder, adultery, etc."[32]

Some natural law principles, however, do not easily lend themselves to incorporation in a public consensus. There are many "relatively complicated human situations in which the good and evil—that is to say, the inherent demands of reason—are not so easily discerned, and the principles of right action are not so evident to the man on the street."[33] In these cases, those who bear special responsibility for the well-being of society also bear responsibility for the particularization of the transcendent principles of natural law in the immanent substance of the public consensus.[34] It is important to remember, however, that although great difficulty may accompany the particularization of natural law principles in these difficult situations, the principles themselves are accessible to human reason. Reason, in this case, is that form of rationality proper to political judgement—i.e., *prudence*—which is "tutored by [both] experience and reflection."[35]

The content of the public consensus thus represents the particularization of the "remote principles of the natural law" in concrete historical circumstances. One may legitimately consider the public consensus to be that dynamic matrix which intervenes between moral principles and legal enactments. The public consensus therefore serves as a mediating agent between the universal moral law and the particular *corpus* of public law which maintains civility, justice, peace, freedom, and unity in a given society at a unique historical moment.

The public consensus derives any authority it may claim to exert over society solely on the basis of its inherent rationality. Murray stated explicitly that "if the public consensus comes into being at all, and wins the assent of the public mind, and actually sets a controlling hand . . . on the political-economic action of society, it is only because its principles have been found . . . to be in accord with reason."[36] The public consensus only includes principles to which all reasonable people will assent; it excludes those elements of the moral law whose authority results solely from their character as revealed truths.

Murray concluded that if there is to be a public consensus in American society, "its formation is a testimony to the slow and subtle operation of that rational dynamism, inherent in human nature, which is called natural law." The process by which society generates this consensus is also "characteristic of natural law thinking." Finally, the source of the authority by which the public consensus directs the actions of society is the same as that which establishes the authority of the natural law—i.e., "the high authority of right reason."[37]

The natural law tradition thus facilitates the formation of a public consensus which would enable all Americans to resist the encroachments of secularist ideologies which aspire to direct this society according to the dictates of a purely immanent social ethic. The dictates of the natural law, while themselves particularized in the substance of the public consensus, provide the transcendent referent which enables the human community to judge its progress toward its ultimate end by an *objective* standard. As a law that is both "timeless and timely," the natural law enables all human persons to participate in the political life of civil society confident that might does not make right, for right exists eternally within nature as the reflection of the perfect rationality of its Creator.

Religion in the Public Forum: Some Practical Applications

Though he recognized the need for a theoretical defense of the Church's political activity, Murray would not neglect "the felt necessities of the time" in order to insulate theory from *praxis*. As he was exploring the moral bases of the Church's political activity, he was simultaneously engaged in the actual practice of forging an American public consensus. Basing his arguments on the principles of politics he derived from the natural law tradition, Murray focussed his attention on two particular issues which have been the subject of great debate in twentieth century America—the question of governmental censorship of literature and the arts, and the constitutionality of state aid to parochial schools.

It was within the context of his discussion of the question of literary and artistic censorship that Murray confronted the important issue of determining the relationship between morality and legality.[38] He believed that many Americans often misunderstood the true meaning of the medieval adage: "Whatever is right ought to be law." They assumed that this principle meant that the state and its coercive power ought to "compel the people to do whatever is right." Murray believed that in the United States, "whenever some good thing needs doing or some evil thing needs to be done away with, the immediate cry is for the arm of the law."[39]

According to Murray, this medieval principle, properly understood, merely implied that "whatever is right ought to be reflected in custom; that is, the moral order ought to be reflected in the habitual order of everyday life and action." In framing the issue in this way, he believed that American society ought to strive, not for the legislation of morality, but for the recognition of "the distinction and relation that obtains between the order of moral law and the order of [human] law or custom."[40] In other words, abstract moral principles do not find their immediate embodiment in human law. Instead, the customs or mores of society play an integral role as the means of mediating the universal to the particular in a moral universe that reflects the unity and harmony of what is right by nature.

In applying these principles within the context of the particular issue of censorship, Murray recognized the seemingly tragic nature of the conflict between the right of the state to censor media of communication and the right of the writer or artist to freedom of expression.[41] Where they contribute to the actualization of human potentialities, both of the aforementioned rights are intrinsically good. Statesmen must therefore carefully consider the jurisprudential norms of rectitude and utility in order to determine the proper manner of establishing a right relationship between the universal and eternal imperatives of the moral law and the contingent imperatives of the human law of a particular time and place.

In general, Murray believed that any constraint of freedom "must be for the sake of freedom"—i.e., "the constraint must create a freedom in another respect." This principle derived its authority from the American *jurisprudential* tradition; it was *not* a universal moral absolute. Murray stated this fact clearly when he wrote that in the United States, "we have constitutionally declared that the presumption is in favor of freedom, and that the advocate of constraint must make a convincing argument for its necessity or utility in the particular case."[42] The *practical* wisdom of the statesman thus determines the justice of censorship laws.

Given this preferential option for freedom in American society, Murray held that any laws sanctioning governmental censorship of literature or the arts must illuminate the unique circumstances which warrant their embodiment in the statutes which the state will enforce with the coercive power at its disposal. Those who would frame such legislation must recognize that "morals and law are differentiated in character, and not coextensive in their functions." They must also recognize that "it is not the function of the legislator to forbid everything that moral law forbids, or to enjoin everything that the moral law enjoins." Legislators must always remember that "the moral law governs the entire order of human conduct, personal and social, [and] it extends even to motivations and interior acts." Human law, on the other hand, "looks only to the public order of human society. . . . [It] touches only external acts, and regards only values that are formally social." Legislation must therefore always demonstrate a cognizance of the fact that "the moral aspirations of the law are minimal."[43]

In the case of censorship laws, the *power* of the state can only legitimately extend to the preservation of public order in society; "society must look to other institutions for the elevation of its moral standards." It is more properly the role of "the Church, the home, the school, and the whole network of voluntary associations" to exercise the moral *authority* necessary to harmonize the mores of society with the imperatives of the natural law. Therefore, the impotence of the human law to coerce morally good behavior compels those who seek public peace to "be tolerant of many evils that morality condemns."[44]

In order to avoid a tragic conflict of values and positively promote the formation of a public consensus which would be relevant to an issue as divisive as that of censorship, Murray argued that all members of society must recognize that "what is commonly imposed by law on all our citizens must be supported by general public opinion, by reasonable consensus of the whole community." This is not to deny that "within a pluralistic society, . . . minority groups have certain definite . . . rights to influence the standards of public morality."[45] These rights, however, are necessarily circumscribed by four principles which Murray considered necessary ingredients in the peaceful solution of this problem.

In proposing his solution to the problem of censorship, Murray noted that (1) "within the larger pluralist society, each minority group has the right to censor for its own members . . . the various media of communications." Conversely, however, (2) "no minority group has the right to demand that government should impose a general censorship...upon any medium of communication . . . according to the special standards held within one group."[46]

Murray also insisted that (3) all minority groups possess the positive entitlement "to work toward the elevation of standards of public morality . . . through the use of methods of persuasion and pacific argument." Finally, (4) he of course precluded from such legitimate means of persuasion "the methods of force, coercion, or violence."[47]

In determining the morality of public censorship of art or literature, legislators must consider how these laws contribute to the preservation and promotion of *public order*. It remains to the Church and other religious organizations, the family, schools, and voluntary associations to promote the *common good* by fostering harmony between the mores of society and that which is right by nature. The question of censorship thus illuminates in a practical manner Murray's understanding of the limited role of human law as a means for promoting public morality. More significantly, it offers a practical lesson in the exercise of political prudence as a factor mediating the imperatives of the natural law to the human law. Ultimately, Murray's approach to the issue of censorship demonstrates how one may perceive the abstract distinction between society and state as operative in the particular circumstances of twentieth century America.

If Murray's approach to the issue of censorship indicates an inclination to limit the role of the state in the affairs of society, his argument for state aid to parochial schools indicates a seemingly incongruous position. We must therefore conduct a careful analysis of his treatment of this second issue in order to determine whether he maintained a consistent method of political reasoning in reaching different conclusions regarding the appropriateness of state action in promoting the common good of society.

The occasion for Murray's protracted entrance into the debate regarding the constitutionality of state aid to parochial schools was the

Supreme Court's adoption of the "Strict Separation" or "No Aid" theory which held that "there must be a strict separation of Church and State, and that government may not constitutionally provide support to religion or religious interests."[48] What Murray found most offensive in the cases in which the Court elaborated this theory was not the results which the decisions effected but rather the "doctrinal quality" of the *absolute* separation of Church and state which the Justices sought to incarnate in American constitutional law.[49]

Murray believed that any jurisprudential theory which incorporated a principle of "absolute separation" of Church and state was as violative of the First Amendment's establishment clause as a constitutional or statutory provision which designated a particular belief system as the religion of the state. By embodying both the Jeffersonian metaphor of an impenetrable "wall" separating Church and state and the Madisonian belief in the purely private nature of religion in the *corpus* of American constitutional law, the Supreme Court "established" as public law the theological principle that "religion is of its nature a personal, private, interior matter of the individual conscience, having no relevance to the public concerns of the state." It was indeed paradoxical, Murray wrote, that "in the effort to prove that 'no establishment of religion' means 'no aid to religion,' the Supreme Court proceed[ed] to establish a religion—James Madison's." What he considered most treacherous about the reasoning behind these decisions, however, was the fact that

> in the name of freedom of religion . . . [the Court] decree[d] that the relations of government to religion are to be controlled by the fundamental tenet of secularism—the social irrelevance of religion, its exclusion from the secular affairs of the City, and its educational system, [and] its relegation to the private forum of conscience.[50]

In arguing that the absolute separation of Church and state forbade any governmental aid to parochial schools, the Court also obliterated the functional relationship that existed between the "establishment" and "free exercise" clauses of the First Amendment. If one removes the theological content of a Deist theory of separation, it is clear that non-establishment makes a valuable contribution to the public peace when combined with such complementary ideas as "the distinction of the ecclesiastical and civil jurisdictions [and] the immunity of conscience from coercion by civil authority in the free exercise of religion." These "principles of peace" are properly political, not theological, principles. In the *Everson* and *McCollum* cases, however, "so far from being instrumental to 'free exercise,' a means relative to an end, the 'establishment' clause (in the meaning of 'no aid to religion') . . . assumed the primacy, the status of an absolute, an end-in-itself." As a result, the "free exercise" clause became "subordinate" and "religious liberty," properly understood, was greatly diminished.[51]

This absolute separation of Church and state also indicated a tendency toward a form of social monism in the order of education. By establishing the principle that although "the child may not be the creature of the state, the school definitely is," the Court created an environment hostile to the operation of religiously-affiliated schools. The Court's decisions also established the principle that the schools' functions "are determined solely by the state" and that "even the child's time in school is owned by the government." By implication, then, "the child has a 'legal duty' to put all this time in on secular subjects," and the parents' right to educate their children is "limited by the exigencies of a 'unifying secularism' that is a constitutional necessity in public education."[52] Such a statement of the exclusive authority of the state in the order of education clearly attempted to deny the Church access to the *res sacra in temporalibus* and therefore restricted her fundamental claim to freedom.

To Murray, this emerging social monism in education was as great an evil as the appendage of Deist theology to the U.S. Constitution. He condemned the Supreme Court's effort to hamper the "religious and civic equality of the American parent and child" by placing burdens on those who seek to exercise their right to religious liberty by choosing educational alternatives to the state-operated public school. He concluded that there would be no truly just solution to the problem of governmental aid to parochial schools "until the parent is moved into the center of the problem, and people stop debating the question in terms of Church and state."[53]

Murray bolstered his argument by noting that "the parochial school fulfills an essentially public function—that of preparing an educated citizenry." Any reasonable person would acknowledge that "because a school may . . . recognize that man is a religious person as well as a civic person and therefore . . . educates him religiously, . . . it does not for this reason cease to be a school, and to fulfill a public function, and to contribute to the general welfare." Murray believed that if the U.S. Constitution required the absolute denial of state aid to parochial schools, then American society would have reached the point at which religion had become "a civic liability, a principle of discrimination in regard of common educational assistance." Such a blatant appropriation of secularist ideology, he argued, is nothing less that "an embarrassment to government itself."[54]

In the final analysis, Murray claimed that the Court's denial of state aid to parochial schools was defective both as a matter of moral principle and in its failure to acknowledge the sociological facts of twentieth century America. On the level of moral principle, the denial of state aid to parochial schools violated the imperative of distributive justice. This moral norm "require[d] that government, in distributing burdens and benefits within the community, should have in view the needs, merits, and capacities of the various groups of citizens and society in general." Murray believed that the principle of absolute separation of Church and state was not in accord with what is right by nature because "the principle of distributive justice would require that a proportionately just measure of public support should be available to such schools as serve the public cause of popular education, whether these schools be specifically religious in their affiliation and orientation, or not."[55]

The Court's rulings also failed to recognize the fact that by the middle of the twentieth century, "American society ha[d] assumed a new pluralist structure" which was neither "vaguely Protestant nor purely secular." Within American society, Catholics and other religious people maintain the integrity of their religious beliefs while they are simultaneously "integrated into its pluralist structure" in which "educational needs and interests . . . [are] public needs and interests at the same time that they remain special to the particular community." Because the state must distribute educational resources proportionately, even where particular religious groups have established a "private" school "system," Murray considered "the denial of all manner of public aid to this kind of school system . . . [to be] an anomaly . . .

[which] represents a failure or a refusal to deal with the facts, with the altered realities of American life."[56]

Murray proposed the concept of "accommodation" as a norm which he believed was appropriate to the adjudication of establishment clause cases, particularly in the area of education. As a people, Americans agree that "government should not undertake responsibility for the care of the sacred order of religious life." We believe that "governmental responsibility is limited to a care for freedom of religion." Such a separation of Church and state does not mean, however, that government must be "hostile or even indifferent to the things of God."[57] Quoting Justice William O. Douglas, Murray wrote that in American society, the state ought to respect "the religious nature of the people and accommodate . . . [its] public service to their spiritual needs."[58]

Murray appreciated the fact that "applying this principle will be difficult." However, its application on a case by case basis, "in an atmosphere of reasonable argument unclouded by passion or prejudice," will actually promote "a more harmonious statement of the full American tradition of right relations between government and religion."[59]

This conclusion in defense of state aid to parochial schools is completely compatible with his position regarding governmental censorship of literature and the arts despite the difference in his conclusions regarding the proper extent of the state's activity. If one transcends the narrow issue of governmental action vs. governmental restraint, it is easy to observe that Murray is completely consistent in his distinction between the state's limited role in promoting public order and society's pursuit of the higher goal of the common good of all its members. In the case of censorship, Murray advocated a limited role for the state (the exercise of power only to preserve public order) and remanded to the other orders of society (the Church, the family, voluntary associations, etc.) the responsibility for "censorship"—i.e., the judgement of art and literature's contribution to the actualization of human potentialities.

In the case of state aid to parochial schools, Murray again stated that responsibility for education can never be *exclusively* in the hands of the state. Even if members of society consent to enfranchise the state with a fiduciary responsibility for *part* of their role in the education of their children, the state can never claim omnicompetence in this area of social life. Consequently, if the state is to distribute its resources for the purpose of education, the principle of distributive justice forbids discrimination on the basis of religious belief when determining the beneficiaries of such grants. To the degree that they provide the education necessary to promote the common good of society, all schools—public and private—should share in the resources which the state has collected through the use of its coercive power: the state cannot legitimately penalize people who espouse particular religious beliefs when it remunerates those who cooperate in the project of civic education.

This analysis of Murray's social criticism and his advocacy of the perennial wisdom of the natural law tradition demonstrates the degree to which his study of the relationship of religion and politics transcended the narrow issue of the juridical relationship between Church and state. He continued his study of the Gelasian Thesis by considering its viability as a source of wisdom for those engaged in the search for solutions to the most practical political problems. Murray's work was clearly influential in the Church's effort to state its teaching in a manner that was relevant to the political experience of the world's peoples in the twentieth century. It therefore remains to be seen whether his political theology remains a source of wisdom for those who continue his project of promoting civic unity and respect for authentic human freedom.

Glossary

conscientia ex lex:
"a lawless conscience;" a conscience that pursues ends which it has chosen for itself without reference to any objective standard of rectitude including the Natural Law.

Distributive justice:
the maintenance of a social order that respects the individual's right to private ownership of property and simultaneously secures the access of all people to an equitable portion of the goods which God has created to be shared by all so that all persons might live in a manner conducive to the actualization of their human potentialities.

principatus sine modo sine lege:
"rule without limit or law"; the exercise of absolute power by a state without accountability to any authority higher than itself.

res sacra in temporalibus:
"a sacred thing among temporal things"; any aspect of life in society which appears primarily to be ordered toward a temporal good but also contributes to the realization of one's supernatural end.

Subsidiarity:
the principle which asserts the right of various sub-political groups to exist and to contribute to the common good of civil society to the extent to which they are capable. This principle also posits the right of the state to assume the exercise of functions proper to sub-political groups when the latter prove incapable of achieving the ends toward which they are naturally ordered.

telos:
"end"; that toward which persons and societies are naturally inclined according to God's eternal plan for Creation.

Discussion Questions

1. Is there a tendency toward secularism in American society which threatens to exclude religious groups from participating in the public life of this country? If so, what can religious people do to counteract this "secularist drift?" If not, what social and political mechanisms exist to secure the freedom of religious groups to contribute to the formation of a public consensus?

2. Is Murray's description of "America's Four Conspiracies" an accurate description of the spiritual forces at work in American society?

3. What "-isms" operate as sources of spiritual animation in American society today?

4. How much civic unity can we reasonably hope to attain in a religiously pluralistic society like the United States? Can we identify any specific substantive elements of a public consensus which would command universal assent in this country?

5. Assess the value of the Natural Law tradition (as described by Murray) as an adequate basis upon which Americans might begin the project of forging a public consensus.

6. Does Murray offer a satisfactory description of the relationship between morality and legality? What political issues, besides censorship, manifest the pressing need to recognize the limited power of the state to codify moral principles?

7. Discuss the strengths and weaknesses of legislative, executive, and judicial efforts to promote governmental accommodation of the beliefs and practices of religious groups in the public life of American society.

Chapter 6

Murray's Political Theology: Accomplishment of the Past, Resource for the Future

FROM THE PRECEDING ANALYSIS, IT OUGHT TO BE EVIDENT THAT JOHN Courtney Murray's political theology was a great source of wisdom for those who sought to explain the proper relationship between the spiritual and temporal societies in the twentieth century. Murray's explanation of the principles of social dualism as well as his application of these principles clarified the Church's role as both a moral critic in the temporal society and as a positive agent promoting the spiritual and temporal welfare of every human person. It seems appropriate at this point to offer a final evaluation of Murray's work and consider its lasting value as an analysis of the history of Catholic political theology and as a resource for those who will continue the effort to explain the relationship between religion and politics in the future.

Murray's Theoretical/Historical Study of the Principles of Social Dualism

Murray's effort to resurrect and re-animate the principles of the Gelasian Thesis was indeed one of his greatest contributions to Catholic social thought in the twentieth century. His study also provided an invaluable explanation of Catholic teaching for those in American society who do not share the Catholic faith but who nevertheless wish to understand the Church's teachings. One may further claim that his study was beneficial to the universal community of political theorists, as he probed the issue of personal integrity in the infinitely complex world of human social existence.

By ultimately focussing his study on the issue of the moral integrity of the individual human person, Murray secured the attention of every thoughtful person who recognizes that rights and duties, freedoms and obligations, adhere to people who possess a fundamental dignity solely on the basis of their humanity. He assumed the inviolable status of this assertion, and he posited its eternal and universal validity in every subsequent effort to understand the moral order in which all people live.

After asserting the fundamental dignity of the human person, he quickly noted that personal integrity does not in any way imply simplicity. He described the complexity of human social existence by characterizing the human person as both an individual and a member of society, as existent in a natural society and created ultimately for a supernatural end. In this statement of the complex existence of the individual moral agent, one may locate Murray's explanation of the universal moral principles which order human social existence as well as the bases for the norms which govern the institutionalization of these principles in particular historical circumstances.

As one observes the development of Murray's political theology, it is obvious that the principles of the Gelasian Thesis assume the status of postulates in any effort to explain the appropriate relationship of religion and politics. He constantly reminded Catholics that they are citizens of two societies, the spiritual and the temporal, that the spiritual possesses a certain primacy by virtue of the higher dignity of its end, and that the promotion of harmony or *concordia* between them is a moral imperative which binds eternally and universally. Without coercing others to assent to this understanding of human social existence, Murray made explicitly clear the Catholic teaching which was both accessible to human reason and confirmed by the revealed Word of God.

In his studies of the application of universal principles in diverse historical circumstances, Murray demonstrated the importance of constant vigilance lest one grow remiss in maintaining the necessary distinction between the universal and the particular. He ably demonstrated that misinterpretations and abuses are never confined to one particular era, nor is an authentic teaching established at once for all times. Though Gelasius I stated the universal and eternal *principles* of Catholic teaching, the *applications* of these principles have been, in turn, distorted (Gregory VII), hierocratic (Boniface VIII), restorative (John of Paris), historicist (Robert Bellarmine), conservative (Leo XIII), and reactionary (Ottaviani, Fenton, *et al.*). Murray's work thus demonstrates the perennial need to determine which elements of Church teaching are universal and which are contingent. By implication, this project also engages the Church in the task of determining the situations in which she is *ecclesia docens*—teaching the principles of the faith—and when she is *ecclesia discens*—seeking the best manner of applying principles in order to minister effectively within the historical and cultural milieu in which she finds herself.

Murray went beyond a description of the imperatives which order the relationship between the spiritual and temporal societies in order to explain the plurality of orders within the temporal society itself. This endeavor enabled him first to emphasize the complexity of the matrix of institutions which impact human persons seeking to actualize both their individual and social potentialities. In describing the structure of the temporal society as a composite of subsidiary institutions, Murray also indicated the need to recognize the limited role of the state in the life of civil society and the necessity of preserving the freedom of the Church to lend her voice to any public discussion of those elements of social life which have the character of *res sacra in temporalibus.*

One may justly credit Murray for promoting a great political-theological advance in his study of the modern appropriation of the medieval principles of the Gelasian Thesis. His research demonstrated great fidelity to the meaning of the original fifth century texts. He was objective beyond reproach in his criticism of such eminent Catholic teachers as Gregory VII, Boniface VIII, and Robert Bellarmine.[1] He also traced very clearly the continuity of authentic Catholic teaching from the fifth century (Gelasius) through the thirteenth century (John of Paris) into the nineteenth and twentieth centuries (Leo XIII).

This theoretical and historical survey, and his statement of the fundamental principles of the Gelasian Thesis, enabled Murray to establish the authentic tenets of Catholic teaching regarding the relationship of religion and politics. The principles of social dualism, as derived from the dictum of Pope Gelasius, represented universal principles of both the divine and natural law. Murray's historical survey demonstrated the important fact that it is impossible to assume that these universal principles can ever find their "ideal" embodiment in the social *praxis* of any particular era. In illuminating the perennial nature of this problem, Murray made an invaluable contribution to all who seek to understand the Catholic faith. He framed the problem of politics in terms of the mediation of the universal and the particular, and he refused to condemn any effort to create a Christian structure of politics so long as that effort recognized the necessary contingency of all particular applications of universal principles.

The Argument for Religious Liberty

Murray's effort to justify the normative value of religious liberty consumed his time and energy for over two decades. By giving almost exclusive attention to this issue, he was able to publish numerous articles which indicate the rather clear development of his thought. He also demonstrated his ability to analyze complicated political and theological tracts and later synthesize his insights into a carefully constructed, logically organized, and doctrinally sound argument for a new articulation of a Catholic teaching which traced its roots to the fifth century.

Murray's religious liberty arguments demonstrate once again his integrity as a scholar. He frankly admitted the failure of his first effort to formulate a new Catholic political theology. He demonstrated his commitment to pursue the truth by continuing his intellectual journey alone, even when opposed by the formidable ecclesiastical power of those who resisted his theological innovations and secured the censorship of his work. During the period in which he ceased publishing articles on the development of Catholic doctrine *vis à vis* religious liberty, Murray maintained a commitment to the belief that no human power could prevent the truth from becoming the norm which guided the teaching of the Church. He could obediently accept this temporary cessation of the publication of his work confident that just as John of Paris corrected the flaws of Boniface's political theology, so others would eventually accept his conclusion that the teachings of Leo XIII and Pius XII clearly provided the theological basis for a rejection of the *thesis/hypothesis* distinction and the affirmation of the normative value of religious liberty.

In addition to demonstrating his scholarly integrity, Murray's study of the normative value of religious liberty provides a concrete example of the appropriate manner of mediating universal theological and ethical principles to their particular embodiment in the contingent dictates of human constitutional and statutory law. In the course of this study, Murray advanced a contemporary understanding of the 13th-century Thomistic description of the nature of law. He described the moral universe as inherently rational in consequence of the perfect rationality of its Creator. He described the two sources of eternal and universal principles which ought to guide human action—the natural law and the divine law—and he stated the source of the human knowledge of these laws—reason and revelation, respectively. Murray also noted the important fact that while the imperatives which emanate from these two sources of law are indeed unchanging, they themselves cannot find immediate embodiment as practical norms in the concrete reality of human social existence. Such a statement was utterly consistent with his entire project of demonstrating the extreme complexity of the moral universe in which we live.

Murray indicated that *practical* norms can never come *immediately* from either revelation or human reason and be valid for all times and places. Abstract theological and ethical principles only find their embodiment within the contingent, positive human and divine laws which guide human behavior at a specific time and place. In the case of political norms which govern the temporal society, an intermediate jurisprudential norm must mediate the universal principles of the natural law to the contingent positive human law. In the case of the practical norms which direct the action and activity of the Church and its members, magisterial teaching mediates the abstract universal principles of the divine law to the positive dictates of Catholic doctrine.

All political theorists who seek to understand the operation of natural law principles in contingent historical circumstances will benefit from a study of Murray's description of the role of jurisprudence as the means of mediating the universal and particular elements of the moral law. In contrast to those who would argue that the criterion of *possibility* ought to govern the immediate codification of abstract principles in historical circumstances, Murray noted that two jurisprudential norms govern the formulation of human law. The first of these norms is that of *rectitude*—i.e., the consistency of a given law with the principles of the natural law which require either action or abstinence on the part of the individual human person. The second norm is that of *utility*—i.e., the necessity or usefulness of a given law for the promotion of public peace. Both of these norms govern the mediation of natural law principles in human law and indicate the authentic contingency of human law, whose principles change according to the contingent nature of the historical period in which they are normative.

Murray's study of the issue of religious liberty is also significant because in his description of the role of jurisprudence in the mediation of the universal and the particular, he not only affirmed the inherent dignity of the temporal society and its governors, but he also renewed his commitment to the promotion of harmony between the two societies. He stated that one of the essential principles of Catholic social teaching is the recognition of the competence of the temporal power to judge the political exigences of contemporary social life. While he repeated the Church's claim to exclusive competence in the determination of the imperatives of the divine law, Murray promoted mutual cooperation between religious and political leaders in the framing of just human laws. He believed that if competent political authorities respected the moral teachings explained by the Church as a participant in the political life of a free society, and if Church leaders respected the ability of civil leaders to estimate properly the degree of coercion necessary to secure public order, then the subsidiary institutions within society would retain the freedom necessary to promote the common good in a stable political environment. Such an understanding of the jurisprudential mediation of moral and civil law obviously does not separate religion and politics. It rather insists that Church leaders forego the attempt to equate moral principles with particular political norms, and it also requires legislators and governors to recognize the contribution of the teaching authority of the Church to the effort to promote of the common good of the temporal society.

In his theoretical defense of the principle of religious liberty, Murray described the complexity of the moral order and the mediation of universal principles in particular circumstances without losing sight of the most important element in the whole *corpus* of his political theology—the fundamental integrity and dignity of the human person. In its final phase, his argument for religious liberty rested nearly exclusively on the fundamental dignity of the human person as moral agent. Murray focussed his attention, not on an abstract notion of "liberty of conscience," but on the personal integrity of all human persons as they seek to *act* on the dictates of their consciences. Again returning to such first principles as the duality of human citizenship and the limited power of the state, Murray ultimately argued that within a mature political community which recognized this structure of the moral universe, the freedom to act according to the dictates of one's conscience and the freedom from being coerced to act against the dictates of one's conscience are indeed fundamental human rights.

Murray's argument in defense of religious liberty represents the summit of his theoretical investigation of the structure of the moral universe and the complex matrix of institutions and imperatives within which individuals must foster the actualization of their natural and supernatural potentialities. In its final stage, this argument synthesized the principles of the Gelasian Thesis, the Thomistic understanding of law, and the humanistic concern for the personal integrity of the individual moral agent. His argument maintained a fidelity to the universal principles of the divine and human laws as well as an awareness of and a responsiveness to those elements of human social existence which establish the *contingent* nature of human law.

Murray's statement of the correct understanding of Catholic teaching regarding Church-state relations could stand as a landmark contribution in its own right. By the conclusion of the Second Vatican Council he had explained the mediation of the universal principles of the Gelasian Thesis within the political environment of the twentieth century in a manner which merited the approbation of the universal Church. His work clearly illuminated the Church's teaching for her own members as well as for those who did not share her faith but sought to understand her doctrine. Murray's genius, however, lay in the fact that he not only established the normative value of religious liberty, but he also envisioned this right as an invitation to the Church and to all religious groups to transcend their own boundaries in order to make a valuable contribution to the welfare of society as a whole.

The Meaning of Religious Liberty in the United States

Murray's attempt to describe the actual manner of Catholic participation in the political life of the United States placed his work in the midst of a public debate involving people both within and outside of the Church. His writings on this subject tend to reflect his own perception of the very different intellectual and religious experiences of those whom he addressed. The arguments which he directed at those within the Church obviously derive their authority from their basis in revealed truths. The arguments which he directed toward those who did not share the Catholic faith made their appeal to rational principles which all reasonable people ought to understand without reference to their particular religious beliefs. These intra- and extra-ecclesial arguments possess a variety of strengths and weaknesses.

Murray's Intra-Ecclesial Argument

Murray's argument in defense of religious liberty as codified in the U.S. Constitution was doctrinally sound and logically consistent. Where he met opposition from others within the Church, this opposition usually grew out of a fear that Murray's defense of the American constitutional order (in which all religious people and groups receive equal justice under law) also implied the equality of all beliefs within the order of truth. Murray denied that the U.S. Constitution endorsed such an understanding of the metaphysical world. He stated that this body of law simply attempted to preserve the public peace in a society in which disagreement over the answers to life's ultimate questions is a social fact.

In the course of the controversy which accompanied the development of his religious liberty argument, Murray and his critics often debated the meaning of Leo XIII's apostolic letter *Longinqua Oceani*. While his critics believed that this letter represented the Pope's indication that the separation of Church and state in the United States was to be considered purely *expedient*, and that religious liberty was a "lesser evil" and tolerable only where it was not possible to establish Catholicism as the religion of the state,[2] Murray steadfastly denied the authenticity of this interpretation and instead argued that no particular legal arrangement could obtain the status of dogma.[3]

It was in response to charges of universalizing the value of religious pluralism and relativizing the value of religious truth that Murray stated explicitly his understanding of the appropriate manner of ordering one's religious and patriotic loyalties. He wrote that he never intended to "erect the American fact of a religiously pluralistic society into a principle," nor did he intend to "erect the American constitutional law which deals with this fact into an ideal." He simply maintained that "the First Amendment, within the American religious, political, and social situation can be defended in principle" and not simply in terms of its expedience. He believed that the First Amendment was a good law because its assumption of state incompetence in religious matters satisfied the imperatives of the Gelasian Thesis which are part of "the transcendental order of truth and justice." The First Amendment was also good law because it satisfied the second norm which Murray used to judge the morality of law—i.e., it effectively provided for the peace "of the temporal community as it actually exists on earth."[4]

The inclusion of many elements of Murray's intra-ecclesial argument in the Second Vatican Council's Declaration on Religious Liberty is testimony to the normative value of this constitutional arrangement in the twentieth century. The Church has since expanded this concern for religious freedom to include a more general patronage of freedom in all of its forms—freedom of speech, press, assembly, political participation, etc.[5]

Murray's Extra-Ecclesial Argument

Murray's explanation of religious liberty as an empowerment for the formation of an American public consensus rooted in a natural law social ethic represents a complicated issue for analysis. Unlike his intra-ecclesial arguments which provided a theoretical basis for social *praxis*, his extra-ecclesial arguments, if they are at all convincing on the level of theory, are still far from becoming the basis for practical political discourse in the United States.

Murray believed that many Americans feared the growing political power of the Catholic Church in this country because they understood the Church's teaching to include the imperative that Catholicism ought to be the religion of the state whenever social conditions rendered such an institutional arrangement possible. This was not an unreasonable conclusion, particularly in an age in which the *thesis/hypothesis* distinction represented the accepted articulation of Catholic teaching regarding Church-state relations. Given the possibility of a Catholic hegemony, Protestants and Other Americans United for Separation of Church and State fought for the absolute separation which the Supreme Court announced in the *Everson* and *McCollum* decisions and which Murray decried as the codification of Deist theological principle.

Murray argued that the absolute separation of Church and state was never the ultimate goal of the framers of the First Amendment. The First Amendment's proscription of Congress' making any law respecting an establishment of religion meant simply that "Congress shall make no law whose effect would be the legal preferment of one religion [defined here as 'particular articles of faith and a particular mode of worship'], with consequent legal subordination of others."[6] Such an interpretation of the First Amendment would clearly allow state "accommodation" of the needs of religious groups, but it would just as clearly prohibit the establishment of a state religion and the governmental repression of heresy envisioned by proponents of the *thesis/hypothesis* distinction. Non-Catholics would have nothing to fear from the Church once Murray succeeded in demonstrating the normative value of religious freedom.

The problem with Murray's extra-ecclesial argument regarding the participation of religious groups in American public life is his underestimation of the degree to which Deist theological principles have found a home in American constitutional law and, more significantly, in an American public philosophy.[7] Murray was correct in arguing that the First Amendment to the U.S. Constitution did not codify the philosophical principles of continental liberalism, particularly the principles of *conscientia ex lex* and *principatus sine modo sine lege*. One must note, however, that if the Constitution does not reflect the principles of continental liberalism, it does bear the mark of British liberal philosophy, particularly that of John Locke.

Murray undertook an extended analysis of John Locke's theory of natural rights, and he endeavored to prove the moral bankruptcy of such a political vision. He correctly noted that Locke's "'state of nature' was a purely imaginary construct," and that the postulation of its existence served only "to explain, in conjunction with the theory of the social contract, the genesis of political society, its form, and the relative rights of government and citizen." Murray concluded that Locke's theory of "the law of nature, the rights of man, and the origins of society are not derived from what is 'real,' from the concrete totality of man's nature as it really is." Instead, the principles of Locke's political theory "are deduced from an abstraction, a fictitious state of nature, a disembodied idea of man."[8]

Relying almost exclusively on Locke's *Second Treatise of Government*, Murray described his political theory in terms of three basic principles: 1) "the inalienability of the rights of the individual to life, liberty, and property, and the limitation of these rights solely by the equal rights of other individuals"; 2) the necessity of popular consent for the institution of government; and 3) "the limitation of governmental power by the 'common good.'" According to Murray, Locke described civil society as a conglomeration of "sociological monads" ("not the product of nature but of artifice") in which the "common good consists merely in the security of each individual in the possession of his property."[9]

Murray was critical of such a description of human social existence because "the premise of Locke's state of nature is a denial that sociality is inherent in the very nature of man." Locke's vision of politics rejected the Aristotelian-Thomistic claim that "society is . . . organized in ascending forms of sociality that are made necessary by, and radicated in, nature itself." Murray concluded that "in Locke's theory, all forms of sociality are purely contractual; they have no deeper basis in the nature of man than a shallow 'reason' that judges them useful."[10] Locke's political theory is therefore not "rational" but "rationalist."

Murray criticized the logical outcome of a political program based on such philosophical premises. In the structure of politics outlined by Locke, there is no "*ordo juris*, and no rights in any recognizable moral sense." Politics becomes simply "a pattern of power relationships—the absolute lordship of one individual balanced against the equally absolute lordship of others." In such a political system, the state is not an institution capable of contributing to the common good of society. The "common good" which this political society pursues "is nothing real in itself . . . but simply a symbol for the quantitative sum of individual goods." Finally, in Locke's political theory, "'right' is not a term relating to a moral order deriving from the essences of things; it is simply a symbol flourished to assure the free functioning of self-interest."[11]

Murray attempted to salvage the American "translation" of Lockean principles by pointing to their compatibility (though not their kinship) with the medieval principles of the natural law tradition. Murray believed that Americans had inherited from Locke a debased form of the "central medieval tradition of the supremacy of law over government." He also believed that through Locke, Americans inherited (again in a debased form) "the medieval principle that sovereignty is 'translated' from the people to the ruler who is responsible to the people . . . and holds title to it only as long as he serves their common good." Finally, Murray believed that the medieval natural law principle of "the right of the people to participate in government" found a place in the American political tradition through the theoretically dubious viaduct of Lockean political theory.[12]

Murray's was an attempt to portray rationalist political thought, especially that of John Locke, as an authentic, although fundamentally flawed and therefore unworthy, cipher of ancient and medieval political principles. This caricature of the theoretical bases of the American Founding, however, is one with which serious scholars must take exception.

There can be no doubt that those who most significantly influenced the framing of the American documents of freedom sought first to establish and defend the rights of individual citizens against the real or potential threat of an absolute monarch or a totalitarian political regime.[13] Those who defended the American claim to independence and the constitutional government established to safeguard that liberty sought primarily to assert the supremacy of law over government, the natural sovereignty of the people, and the right to popular participation in public affairs. These Founders, however, couched their defense of these principles in language that was authentically Lockean and effectively devoid of medieval philosophical constructs.

Jefferson's Declaration of Independence clearly reflects the three elements of Locke's political philosophy (as Murray described it). First, he spoke of the inalienable rights of the "sociological monads" who comprise society when he affirmed in his famous dictum that "we hold these truths to be self-evident: that all men are created equal; that they are endowed by their Creator with certain inalienable rights; [and] that among these are life, liberty, and the pursuit of happiness." He described the artificial and contractual nature of the state when he wrote that "governments are instituted among men, deriving their just powers from the consent of the governed." Finally, he echoed the Lockean principle that the powers of government may only legitimately extend to the promotion of the common good (defined here as the sum total of individual interests) when he stated that "whenever any form of government becomes destructive of these ends, it is the right of the people to alter or abolish it, and to institute new governments" in a manner that "to them shall seem most likely to effect their safety and happiness."[14]

James Madison also advanced arguments which justified the American system of government in terms more reminiscent of the idiom of the Enlightenment than that of the ancient and medieval natural law thinkers. While Madison's writings do not reflect Lockean political principles as literally as Jefferson's do, there is no doubt that he considered the problem of politics in much the same terms as the British Empiricist.

Like Locke, Madison understood the problem of politics to be the promotion of a common good which was simply the quantitative sum of individual interests. Madison believed that "the government in general should have a common interest with the people." It should "deriv[e] its energy from the will of society, and operat[e] . . . in the interest of society." Finally, it should take as its *first object* "the protection of different and unequal faculties of acquiring property."[15]

Madison regarded the citizens of such a political society as "sociological monads" who expected the state to protect their lives and liberties in order that they might acquire more property. The concept of "civic virtue" and the location of such a moral element of political life in the citizenry would have been totally alien to Madison's political thinking. If he were to speak of "virtue" at all, the *locus* of such virtue would be in the people's elected officials. This virtue, however, bears absolutely no resemblance to an Aristotelian-Thomistic concept of virtue. Rather, Madison considered virtue to be the public officials' recognition of their accountability as "organs of the national will." No conception of the "good life" nor any understanding of what is right by nature impels them to be virtuous. Rather, "duty, gratitude, interest, [and] ambition itself are the cords by which they will be bound to fidelity and sympathy with the great mass of the people."[16]

The operative terms of the Madisonian structure of politics are thus "interest," "will," and "property." This is in sharp contrast to Murray's understanding of politics which incorporates as first principles "freedom," "reason," and "justice." The constitutional structure which Jefferson, Madison, and others established in the United States provides the political freedom and civic equality necessary for reasonable and conscientious citizens like Murray to convince their fellow-citizens of the rationality of a social ethic derived from the moral principles of the natural law tradition. This does not imply, however, that such a political system may necessarily locate its philosophical bases in such a social ethic, nor ought it imply that the system, its Founders, or their intellectual ancestors are ciphers (however imperfect) of such a philosophical tradition.

The American political system cannot locate its philosophical or theoretical bases (either directly or indirectly) in the ancient and medieval natural law tradition. Its principal Founders trace their own intellectual heritage to the political theory of the Enlightenment, particularly that of John Locke. This fact does not render Murray's own political project irrelevant to or incapable of implementation in the American constitutional structure. It does, however, identify the political thought of Jefferson and Madison as inimical to a structure of politics which emanates from the natural law tradition and reflects the principles of social dualism. Such an understanding of the thought of American Founders must not discourage those who seek to implement the wisdom of Murray's political theology in the United States. It should, however, indicate the enormity of the project and the necessity of civility in any attempt to secure its implementation.

Conclusion

John Courtney Murray's political-theological investigations are indeed both a significant accomplishment of the past and an extraordinary resource for the future. His re-statement of the principles of the Gelasian Thesis and his critique of their application within the context of medieval, modern, and contemporary political history demonstrate an outstanding commitment to the eternal wisdom of the Church's Tradition and an equally loving concern that the Church always preserve that Tradition by carefully distinguishing universal principles from the contingent elements of their application in particular historical circumstances.

It is probably true that most people associate the name of John Courtney Murray with the Church's Declaration on Religious Liberty. Such a close identification of Murray and that momentous document is testimony not only to his contribution to the Second Vatican Council itself but more importantly to the significance of his theological investigations into the normative value of religious liberty which commanded his attention for over a quarter of a century.

In the course of his study, Murray differentiated the universal and the particular in a manner that reflected his fidelity to the Tradition of the Church as well as his cognizance of the social facts of the twentieth century. He completed an analysis of the complex nature of human social existence, and he invited all people to realize the fullness of their humanity in both the spiritual and temporal societies.

Murray ultimately affirmed the normative value of religious liberty within such a complex social matrix by celebrating the fundamental dignity and value of the human person. This recognition and explicit statement of the dignity of the human person as moral agent may be the most significant element of Murray's political theology. By affirming each individual's moral integrity, Murray asserted that it is the fundamental right of every person to become fully human within both the spiritual and temporal societies free from any external coercion on the part of the state. He also derived from this principle of moral integrity the social-ethical imperative that all people, whatever their religious convictions, have the right to participate in the public discourse of the particular society in which they live. The dignity of the human person establishes the particular imperative that all civil laws must secure the consent of the governed and all people must share equitably in the distribution of society's resources.

Were Murray's reclamation of the Gelasian Thesis, his defense of the principle of religious liberty, and his justification of the participation of all religious people and groups in the formation of an American public consensus to mark the boundaries of his contribution to American Catholic social ethics, then he would justly merit the distinction of being honored as an outstanding theologian. American Catholics best honor this great thinker, however, when they devote their efforts to the contemporary project of translating his works into a resource for the future.

Murray's political-theological project represents an invitation to recognize that the dualistic structure of human social existence ought not to establish barriers between those who believe in a supernatural end and those who do not, or between those who recognize the Church's exclusive authority in the spiritual society and those who do not. Murray's project is rather an invitation to establish community on the highest level of unity possible given the ever-emerging insight of human persons regarding the means available for the formation of a society whose basis in justice will ultimately be transcended by the love which all human persons ought to have for one another.

This vision of human community is indeed a challenging imperative. It is not, however, an abstract "ideal." Murray's vision is grounded in reality—a reality that can only experience progress as a result of the cooperative effort to promote insight into the true bases of civic unity. Unlike modern political theorists for whom politics represents the containment of violence and the immunity of individuals from restraint in the pursuit of interests and ends which they choose for themselves, Murray's vision of politics considered such un-bridled individualism to be the disintegration of politics. The civic unity which facilitates the political organization of a regime is not the product of fear or interest, but rather the result of a natural inclination to become fully human in a social dimension that is as integral to human nature as one's spiritual, intellectual, and physical capacities.

Murray recognized in the natural law tradition a philosophical system which affirmed the essential rationality of creation and the uni-versal and eternal imperative which challenges all persons to become fully human according to an eternal standard which reflects the ratio-nality of its Creator. His understanding of this tradition also chal-lenged the Church to witness to the universal accessibility of natural law principles by reaffirming the inherent dignity of the human person as moral agent and by forswearing an exclusive role as a guardian or cipher of this tradition. If the principles of the natural law are indeed accessible to all human persons by virtue of their innate rationality, then all people must undertake the project of understanding every form of human experience before making a judgement or decision in the effort to achieve greater insight into the unity which is the ultimate end of human society.

As a resource for the future, Murray's political-theological proj-ect indicates that contemporary society is in the midst of a "Catholic moment." This Catholic moment, however, is not an opportunity for the Catholic Church to impose unity where unity does not exist. This Catholic moment is not even an opportunity for the Church to cele-brate triumphantly the final diremption of the politics of modernity as it witnesses the historical manifestation of the inevitable failure of so-cial *praxis* which proceeds from a mistaken understanding of human nature and a de-humanizing totalitarian ideology.

The present moment is Catholic because of the freedom that cur-rently exists to establish community on the basis of universal princi-ples of justice and peace. The present moment is Catholic because human persons in the twentieth century have taken cognizance of their dignity as moral agents who are capable of insight into the nature of politics as a science and an art which promotes the actualization of human potentialities. The present moment is Catholic because while the world possesses the resources to destroy human existence, it also possesses the resources to promote that unity which is peace.

John Courtney Murray's vision of politics is hopeful but not naive. It recognizes that while there is currently the potential for a unity greater than that which human persons have ever experienced, there is also a great need to actualize this potentiality. For American Catholics, the project of promoting that unity begins here and now, in the United States. American Catholics work for justice, not when they measure the degree to which the civil law conforms to the natural law, but when they contribute to and promote the dialogue which seeks consensus regarding the best means of protecting and promoting human rights in all of their multi-faceted dimensions. They defend freedom, not simply by restraining the power of government but by empowering all orders of society to exercise those rights which they claim to possess against the coercive power of the state. Finally, they promote peace, not only by opposing violence in all of its manifestations, but also by seeking the unity and integration of all persons in a society in which people treat each other with respect, justice, and ultimately love.

This task is exceedingly difficult in the complex society in which we live. In the person of John Courtney Murray, we may recognize a human being who accepted and understood the world as it is, in order to begin the project of making it the world that it can be.

Glossary

ecclesia discens: "the Church learning."

ecclesia docens: "the Church teaching."

Longinqua Oceani: apostolic letter addressed by Leo XIII to the Church in the United States in 1895 warning against the danger of considering the separation of Church and state as it existed in this country to be the "ideal" form of Church-state relations.

Discussion Questions

1. Describe the accomplishments of John Courtney Murray as a theologian, political theorist, philosopher, and historian.

2. What questions regarding the relationship between religion and politics remain as part of John Courtney Murray's "unfinished agenda?"

3. Do you agree with Murray's assertion that the Founders of the American regime understood the separation of Church and state to mean something fundamentally different from the continental liberal understanding of this term?

4. Is the American political system founded on philosophical principles that are more closely akin to those of ancient and medieval or Enlightenment political theorists?

Appendix A

An Analysis of Some Interpretations of Murray's Political Theology

THE CHALLENGE OF APPROPRIATING JOHN COURTNEY MURRAY'S POLITI-cal wisdom has been taken up by scholars who have explored the relevance of his political theology to the American regime in the years following the Second Vatican Council. The first significant evaluation of Murray's work (apart from that of his contemporary critics) was not favorable. In recent years, however, a growing number of political theorists and theologians have recognized the value of Murray's work as a great source of wisdom for those who would explain the relationship that ought to exist between the spiritual and temporal societies.

As early as 1965, *E.A. Goerner* criticized Murray's attempt to situate his political thought within the natural law tradition. It was Goerner's contention that "political philosophy historically accepted the task of discovering the order among the variations, and that required the adumbration of the best regime." In his insistence on the contingency of human law and the ever-changing character of the political relationship, however, Murray denied "the possibility of a philosophical typology of regimes." He had "eschew[ed] the work of discerning the structure of the *'optimum genus reipublicae.'*" Therefore, though Murray claimed a commitment to "the tradition of natural law as the basis of free and ordered political life," he nevertheless "abandon[ed] what had always been considered integral to it: a theory of regimes."[1]

Goerner's conclusion was that Murray's political theology is best described as "historicist." He claimed that what Murray described as "intentions of nature" (e.g., "freedom, authority, equality, self-government, the governors-governed relationship"), were merely "abstract formalisms." His failure to produce a theory of regimes "excludes the possibility of the rational articulation of prophetic judgement on any regime." Murray's denial of "not only the historical existence, but even the noetic possibility of an Ideal Republic of Truth and Justice" leads to a "curious demoralization of politics." Finally, his denial of "the possibility of a relevant comprehensive standard [of judgement] continually tends to reduce the concern of politics to mere housekeeping functions."[2]

John A. Rohr later attempted to defend Murray's political theology from Goerner's charges of "historicism." He argued that the term "'historicism' implies an abandonment of transcendental principles in favor of accepting whatever *is* as normative."[3] Such an accusation could never apply to Murray. Though it is indeed true (as Goerner noted) that Murray rejected a typology of regimes and insisted that democracy "is presently man's best, and possibly last, hope of human freedom,"[4] it is also true that Murray made this statement on the basis of democracy's compatibility with two transtemporal principles of the universal moral law. Specifically, Murray affirmed the normative value of democratic government on the basis of its ability to guarantee 1) the freedom of the Church and 2) the security of "the legitimate freedom of the people."[5] Rohr was willing to concede that Goerner's criticism may be "quite sound from the viewpoint of political theory," but he insisted that Goerner "misses the point of what Murray was really doing"—i.e., attempting "to win an argument that defended his nation's institutions in the light of his Church's principles."[6]

I believe that Rohr was far too deferential to Goerner's critique of Murray's political theology. The mere absence of a typology of regimes ought not to exclude Murray from a place in the natural law tradition. Throughout the history of political theory, discrepancies have always existed in the various typologies which theorists have produced, and these discrepancies have always been of a contingent nature. What is of greater significance is the fact that each typology differs only in its estimation of the degree to which each regime *approximates* the establishment of a just political society. One ought to conclude, therefore, that Murray's omission of a typology of regimes is due to his belief that among the types of regimes known in the twentieth century, democracy is the *only* one which reasonably approximates the moral imperatives of a Christian structure of politics. It is therefore ludicrous to exclude Murray from the natural law tradition simply on the basis of an absence of a typology of regimes in his political theology.

Goerner might not have objected so vigorously to Murray's understanding of the contingency of human law and constitutional structures if he were to have enlarged his definition of "regime." He seems to have equated the terms "regime" and "state" in a manner which neglected Murray's own distinction between "society" and "state." In Goerner's moral universe, the term "regime" seems to include only the narrow relationship between ruler and ruled. This would correspond to the political relationship between the individual and the state in Murray's political theology. If Goerner had envisioned the term "regime" to include the individual's relationship to the economic, cultural, religious, educational, and other subsidiary orders in the temporal society (in addition to the individual-state relationship), he might have recognized the wisdom of Murray's statement that the universal nature of the principles which govern all social relationships do not change despite the natural contingency of their institutionalization in particular historical circumstances. Murray always affirmed the existence of universal moral truths despite his denial of the "historical existence" or "noetic possibility" of an "ideal" relationship between ruler and ruled.

Charles E. Curran has also attempted to assess the value of Murray's contribution to American Catholic social ethics. He has expressed admiration for Murray's demonstration of the compatibility of "Catholicism and the American political ethos." He has also praised "Murray's apology for full Catholic acceptance and participation in the American political system," and he has noted that "Murray was one of the first Roman Catholic theologians to recognize the importance of historical mindedness and to employ such a concept in his methodology." Curran insists, however, that "Murray's work is also open to criticism."[7]

Curran contends that Murray's theological idiom, which includes the traditional distinction between the natural and supernatural orders, would be foreign to many contemporary theologians "who call for a more integral approach" and who believe that "the distinction between the natural and the supernatural does not exist as an historical reality [but] at best . . . is only an abstract concept."[8] He also criticizes Murray's failure to "give enough significance to the role of the gospel and of the mystery of Christ in the political and social orders of human existence." Curran believes that Murray has failed to appreciate fully "the reality of sin and its influence on human existence in the temporal sphere." In sum, Murray's political theology neglects the important "need for a change of heart on the part of all individuals in order to bring about peace and justice in our world."[9]

These criticisms are valid if one imagines Murray's audience to have been limited to the Catholic theological community. Were this the case, Murray could have turned exclusively to revealed truths in order to find the authoritative bases of his arguments. He often recognized the necessity of appealing exclusively to *reason*, however, because many of his arguments were intended to persuade those who did not believe in the existence of a supernatural world, the mystery of Christ, or the need for personal conversion. If Murray is guilty of failing to emphasize these revealed truths, such a delict is testimony to his effort to promote civic unity and public peace among all members of society—including those who denied or doubted the existence, attributes, and salvific purpose of God.

Curran is on safer grounds when he criticizes Murray's "bold assertion that the American civic consensus is ultimately grounded only on natural law."[10] He correctly notes that such an assertion implies an assent to "epistemological and metaphysical presuppositions" which do not even command unanimity within the community of American Catholic theologians. In a similar vein, he is correct in noting that Murray left himself "open to the charge of reading into the minds of the founding fathers . . . a natural law mentality." This was clearly not the case as Jefferson's and Madison's rationalist writings prove. Further, it is not enough to say that Murray's venture into American political theory "merely attempts to give a Catholic interpretation of the American proposition," for Murray's "apologetic and polemical purpose" actually confuses the true nature of the American Founding.[11]

Curran also believes that Murray's interpretation of the encyclicals of Leo XIII is also open to criticism. He states that "Murray's interpretation of Pope Leo XIII is ingenious in its distinction among the doctrinal, the polemical, and the historical aspects of the pope's teaching." However, he questions whether "Leo XIII would recognize himself in the picture drawn by Murray!"[12]

On this point, I must take exception with Curran's analysis, for I believe that Murray's restoration of the ancient principles of the Gelasian Thesis and his analysis of the political theory of John of Paris provided an effective standard which enabled him to judge what is universal, contingent, and polemic in all subsequent efforts to state the appropriate relationship between religion and politics, including those of Leo XIII. Further, it should come as no surprise that Leo might not recognize his teaching in its application in the twentieth century, for the one political environment in which the principles of social dualism were being applied was very different from the other. (Gelasius I would not recognize himself in the portrait drawn by Murray either, but that fact should not in itself indicate a lack of fidelity to the principles he articulated, but rather witness to the differences in the historical periods in which the principles were applied.)

Curran concludes that although "serious criticisms can and should be made" regarding his political theology, Murray nevertheless remains "the most outstanding Catholic theologian in the United States in this century."[13]

In addition to these assessments of Murray's personal contributions to Catholic theology, there has also recently been a renewal of the debate surrounding the role of religion in the public life of American society, and many authors, especially Catholic theologians, are either attempting to make Murray's political theology relevant to the contemporary political environment or even going so far as to invoke his name in order to establish the authoritative nature of their own arguments. One of the principal issues in this debate is the possibility of establishing an "American public theology" which would incorporate truths revealed in Scripture as part of the public discourse. These "public theologians" are both interpreters and critics of Murray's political theology, and therefore one must consider whether their works are consistent with Murray's and also (perhaps more fundamentally) whether they even consider Murray's work to be adequate to societal needs in the last decade of the twentieth century.

John A. Coleman was one of the first authors to describe Murray as an American "public theologian."[14] However, Coleman is critical of Murray's exclusion of biblical imagery in his consideration of the traditions which contribute to American self-understanding. According to Coleman, "republican theory, biblical religion, and the public philosophy of Enlightenment liberalism" have all played significant roles in the public life of this country, but Murray's works reveal an explicit "refusal to evoke biblical symbols for the American self-understanding."[15] Coleman predicted that this methodological decision would have devastating consequences for Murray's "public theology."

Coleman noted that Murray's exclusion of biblical imagery reflects his "bias toward liberty at the expense of justice." His attempt "to correct this bias by explicit appeal to the tradition of classic republican theory" was insufficient, for the tradition of republican virtue "is presently such a tenuous force in American life that it does little to reorient our received liberalism in the direction of a vivid concern for the priority of the common good over individual interest."[16]

While Coleman is correct in his assessment of the impotence of classical republicanism to promote the priority of the common good, it is also not likely that an appeal to biblical imagery will fare any better as a means of promoting justice in a religiously pluralistic society. In a nation in which a significant portion of the population would not admit the truth of revealed principles, in which serious sectarian divisions prevent ecumenical cooperation in the implementation of social norms derived from Scripture, and in which people belonging to the same religious tradition dispute the meaning of moral norms derived from Scripture, it necessarily falls to the tradition of reason to promote the common good as an end of greater value than personal interest. While it may promote the cause of freedom in a manner that obscures the value of justice, the principle of *suum cuique* may indeed be the only possible basis from which to begin the construction of a public consensus which recognizes the priority of the common good over individual interests.

Coleman believes that another weakness of Murray's political theology lies precisely in "his failure to admit that his own theory of natural law rests on particularistic Catholic theological principles and theories which do not command widespread allegiance." This criticism appears to overlook Murray's painstaking effort to demonstrate the inherent rationality of the natural law tradition. On numerous occasions Murray appealed only to *reason* to explain systematically the metaphysical, epistemological, and ethical bases of the natural law tradition. His understanding of the essential elements of the natural law tradition—i.e., *suum cuique* and "Justice is to be done and injustice avoided"—includes nothing that may be considered specifically Catholic. It might be more appropriate in this case for Coleman to concede that he himself is among those to whom "the natural law has often seemed more Catholic than natural."[17]

Coleman's final criticism of Murray's political theology is that its idiom of rationality is "unable to evoke the rich, polyvalent power of religious symbolism." If the tradition of Enlightenment liberalism "possesses little power to stir human hearts and minds to sacrifice, service, and deep love of community," and if there is little hope for "a vigorous retrieval . . . [and] understanding of republican theory and virtue," then "the tradition of biblical religion seems the most potent symbolic resource we possess to address the sense of drift in American identity and purpose."[18] This criticism correctly identifies a significant problem inherent in Murray's political-theological project. However, it is also difficult to estimate the extent to which biblical imagery can be expected to function as a force of social cohesion in a religiously pluralistic society.

Another participant in the public theology debate, *Robin Lovin*, believes that "Murray's unfinished agenda . . . includes a rethinking of the distinction between society and state and thus of the role of the Church and the theologian in the social-political sphere." Within the context of this project, Lovin would include the explicit recognition of the "theological foundations beneath the structure of our constitutional system." Lovin asserts that "completing this part of Murray's agenda requires nothing radically new," for the original existence and presence of "the biblical tradition in American culture is an invaluable resource" in the continued effort to protect and promote human rights.[19]

Lovin is correct in identifying the perennial need to reconsider the relationship between society and state and the role of religion in that matrix. This project will encounter immediate and intense criticism, however, if one intransigently insists on the recognition of alleged "theological bases" of the American Founding.

There have been numerous attempts to demonstrate the influence of religious leaders in the period of the American Founding. Nevertheless, one may glean from the documentary evidence only an indication of the *immediate* influence of the Deist philosophy of those statesmen who exercised the most significant roles in the establishment of the American constitutional structure.[20] Lovin's project of promoting respect for human rights by empowering religious groups to participate in public dialogue is indeed *compatible* with Murray's political theology, but again, its call for the recognition of particularized religious symbols as integral elements in the public debate will likely encounter significant resistance in the political environment of our religiously pluralistic society.

David Hollenbach believes that Murray's assumption of the existence of "a public philosophy and a public language for moral discourse common to all Americans . . . is no longer acceptable." It is his contention that "American Catholics need to move beyond an approach to public questions based on Murray's version of the public philosophy to a formulation of a *public theology* which attempts to illuminate the urgent moral questions of our time through explicit use of the great symbols and doctrines of the Christian faith."[21]

Hollenbach offers a balanced approach to the integration of theological and philosophical principles in public discourse. He defines "public theology" as "the effort to discover and communicate the socially significant meanings of Christian symbols and tradition." "Public philosophy," on the other hand, is "the effort to discover and communicate the significant meanings of the common social and political experience in our pluralistic culture." He believes that the task facing American Catholics is to discover "the relationship between these two spheres of meaning and . . . the relationship between the moral norms that these meanings imply." This task is immediately urgent for

> without such reflection public theology will lose contact with the ways God is actively present *in the contemporary social world*...[and] public philosophy risks uncritical affirmation of the categories of contemporary culture and uncritical appropriation of cultural biases which are in contradiction with the moral content of the Christian faith.[22]

Among those who first investigated this problem of incorporating particularized theological symbolism into public discourse, Hollenbach offers a reasonable plan for its accomplishment. His balanced treatment of the issue of integrating philosophy and theology in public recognizes that "both are undoubtedly partially correct and both . . . are undoubtedly indispensable, . . . [but] neither . . . however, is self-evidently complete in itself." He envisions the project of their integration as a constituent element of the "growing end" of Murray's political theology, but he also insists that "the Catholic community in the United States need not wait for such advances in order to speak and act in the public domain."[23]

Hollenbach never offers particular examples of the efficacy of this integration of religious symbolism in public discourse. His expectations of the possibility of an American public theology also seem a bit too optimistic in the absence of any recent advances in the articulation of an American public consensus. However, Hollenbach's position does faithfully reflect Murray's concern for civility in public discourse, and he conscientiously continues Murray's project of probing all avenues of communication which might possibly promote that higher unity which is the natural *telos* of all human persons.

Perhaps the most thorough examination of Murray's contribution to the search for an American public theology is that of *Robert McElroy* who incorporates this idea into the very title of his analysis of Murray's work (i.e., *The Search for an American Public Theology: The Contribution of John Courtney Murray*). McElroy successfully outlines Murray's critique of the secularization of society, his description of the nature of the public consensus, and his program for renewing and restructuring the domestic and international orders. McElroy's greatest contribution to the "public theology" debate, however, is his analysis of Murray's methodological approach to political theology.

McElroy correctly noted that Murray's distinction of natural law principles and particular imperatives of the Catholic understanding of divine law does not in any way generate "a dualistic mode of thinking about the world," nor does it erect "an impenetrable barrier between the sacred and the secular." He believes that Murray's assertion of the primacy of the spiritual ought to promote a harmonious rather than a discordant synthesis of the two laws, for "the superiority of Christian ethics over natural ethics is a superiority of horizon and motivation, not a superiority of action or behavior."[24]

McElroy does not completely exclude religious symbolism from public discourse, nor does he believe that Murray's political theology requires such an exclusion. He believes simply that American religious pluralism currently precludes the effectiveness of basing a public consensus on truths which derive their authority solely from an act of faith. In a manner that is completely consistent with Murray's political theology and which would most effectively integrate particularized religious symbolism into public discourse, McElroy writes that "Scripture and sectarian tradition can indeed add richness, texture, and inspiration to a public theology, but they should always be employed in a way which enhances and brings out the meaning implicit in natural theology." McElroy best captures the spirit of Murray's vision of the role of religion in public discourse when he writes that "biblical and religious claims which cannot be substantiated by independent recourse to natural law should have no place in a contemporary public theology."[25]

Of all of the analyses and interpretations of Murray's political theology, perhaps the most comprehensive and incisive is that of *J. Leon Hooper*. Hooper has not limited his analysis to a differentiation of the idiom appropriate to the sacred and secular societies or to the practical question of the role of theological discourse in the formation of a public consensus. His analysis attempts the "higher synthesis" which Murray envisioned immediately following the promulgation of the Declaration on Religious Liberty.

The unique quality of Hooper's analysis is his explication of the influence of Bernard Lonergan's cognitional theory on Murray's own methodological approach to the question of the relationship of religion and politics. Rather than perceiving the principles of natural and divine law as static and unchanging, it is Hooper's contention that (influenced by Lonergan's cognitional theory) Murray eventually recognized that in the process of moral and political reasoning, "respect for human dignity" requires that "attentiveness, intelligence, reasonableness, and responsibility" must characterize "the generation of new insights and inclusive perspectives." Such respect facilitates the harmonious integration of all forms of pluralism—religious, ethnic, racial, etc. so that "disparate peoples who have been thrown together can be constituted as a people."[26]

Hooper believes that in developing his later understanding of the principles of the Gelasian Thesis, Murray incorporated Lonergan's cognitional concepts of experiencing, understanding, judging, and deciding into his explanation of the task of the "theological social ethician."[27] According to Hooper, Murray's political theology reflects an awareness of the need for the Church and civil society to foster mutual cooperation "in the prudential processes of particular determination, [and] the formation of mediating insights by which both societies can come to common judgements of fact and judgements of value." All who would participate in this dialogue (from which judgements regarding the nature of Truth would emerge) must have equal access and give equal measure of assent to its theological or philosophical idiom, for once "an institution, a social subgroup, or a society becomes blinded to the necessity of, and forgoes, public discussion, then it will be buried under its own lack of insight."[28]

Hooper's understanding of Murray's method of social-ethical reasoning also includes a discussion of the emergence of insight in the realm of those "general value commitments . . . for which we as persons are willing to suffer and die." These principles transcend particular ethical judgements, and although they must "continually reenter the public discussion, . . . this realm of general value discussion must be kept distinct from the first [i.e., *particular* ethical judgements], lest our loves die amid conflict and our ability to respond to the particular historical world in which we live be blinded by our theories."[29] Concrete ethical and general value judgements thus share the same process of determination—experiencing, understanding, judging, and deciding--as well as the same authorization principle—the assent of a society that has reached this emergent state of insight.

According to Hooper, the logical outcome of Murray's political theology is "a confrontation with the God who acts in history." This experience of God, if it is to represent a collective experience of a political community, cannot occur as the result of the sectarian evangelization of an institutional Church. Rather, it must be the result of a collective moral judgement of Truth. In order to facilitate a people's individual and collective experience of the God who is their Author, the Church must surrender any claim to exclusive authority in the public judgement of Truth. Hooper offers the most compelling answer to the question of the role of a particularized theology in public discourse when he writes that

> if the Church is to follow the God who redeems, thereby being true to its own mission and also true to the core consciousness of human society, it has to surrender its own group biases (hidden as those might be behind institutional and theological theories and symbols), while at the same time maintaining its own self-consciousness as a people who witness to God's historical presence.[30]

Hooper has thus proposed the means for taking Murray's call for public ecclesiastical engagement in the temporal world and for a higher synthesis of the imperatives of the sacred and secular societies to its ultimate conclusion. His interpretation of Murray's political theology is universalist in its outlook while it simultaneously preserves the Church's unique identity as a society instituted by Christ. He recognizes in Murray's political theology a vision of a Church which invites all human persons to journey together toward greater collective insight and the ultimate actualization of human nature. As he correctly points out, this collective insight is the result of a communal participation in experiencing, understanding, judging, and deciding. The Church's ministry will be most effective when all people recognize that this is a journey to which the entire human community is invited and from which no one may be excluded.

Hooper's analysis offers an optimistic outlook for the future project of forming a public consensus that progressively encounters through the media of both reason and revelation the God who is the Alpha and Omega of human existence. His project is not naive to the conflict and controversy which necessarily accompany the emergence of insight into the ultimate destiny of the human person. It rather provides an effective lens through which one may analyze the differences of opinion which characterize the contemporary Catholic effort to appropriate the political and theological wisdom of John Courtney Murray in the last decade of the twentieth century. Hooper's work provides an excellent introduction for anyone who would study the manner in which Murray's work has now itself become a topic of discussion as the dialectical process of emerging insight continues and others assume responsibility for continuing his life-work.

J. Bryan Hehir has also won widespread acclaim as a political scientist and theologian whose contributions to Catholic social thought are "comparable to the best of John Courtney Murray's analyses of the subject."[31] Hehir's approach to political-theological issues mirrors Murray's in many ways, for his analysis always appeals to reason when it attempts to persuade in the context of a religiously pluralistic society. Like Murray, he also eschews particularized religious symbolism when such symbols do not appeal to the common experience of those to whom he addresses his arguments.

In determining "which mode of public discourse will most faithfully and effectively draw upon the resources of the Catholic tradition and project its vision and values into public-policy debate," Hehir believes that the increasingly complex and interdependent structure of institutional relationships on the national and international levels requires "systematic solutions which are persuasive for a multiplicity of actors with widely varying 'faith visions.'" Particularized theological symbols may not be persuasive in such environments, and therefore

> the complexity of the major social issues we face, combined with the need to enlist allies who must be persuaded of both the justice and feasibility of specific proposals, requires the sophisticated structure of the kind of *philosophically* rigorous social ethic which the Catholic tradition has provided in the past.[32]

This public philosophical discourse, however, must always remain cognizant of its "growing edge"—i.e., the "continual adaptation of [its] style and structure . . . to new conditions and new questions . . . which needs to be undertaken in light of the new context of increasing interdependence and new forms of human rights claims."[33]

It is from this perspective of the "growing edge" of public philosophy that Hehir considers Murray's works to be simultaneously "a resource for the future as well as an accomplishment of the past." Hehir recognizes that the Church today must address "issues which have changed dramatically since Murray wrote." He also inquires, nevertheless, "to see if Murray's analysis will help us" to find solutions to today's social problems.[34]

Hehir has offered an analysis of the complicated issue of abortion as one example of an attempt to apply Murray's political theology in the contemporary American political environment. Obviously, in discussing the role of religion in public life, the issue of abortion looms as perhaps "the single most fevered and volatile question that inescapably joins religion and politics."[35] Hehir considers the omission of any consideration of this issue in Murray's works to be surprising (given the volatile nature of the subject) but also indicative of "how fast and how profoundly the status of this question shifted in American law and politics." Despite the absence of any explicit reference to abortion in the Murray *corpus*, Hehir believes that "Murray's analysis of the relationship of the civil law and the moral law has implications for both the pro-choice and pro-life positions."[36]

Hehir appropriates Murray's theoretical arguments circumscribing the legitimacy of censorship laws as a great source of wisdom in the effort to determine the appropriate relationship between morality and legality within the context of the abortion debate. Specifically, he states that pro-choice advocates must admit that "a definition of the abortion decision as purely private" would effectively "emasculat[e] the moral authority of the state in other important areas of social and civil conflict." On the other hand, "the consent principle" seems to challenge pro-life advocates to recognize both that it is currently unlikely "that the totality of the Catholic position could be embodied in the civil law," and that it is also incumbent upon them to convince Americans that legislation protecting the lives of the unborn is necessary for the preservation of public order because "permissive abortion policies threaten the very fabric of the society which allows them." It appears to be Hehir's hope that "when we do address the scope of a proposed new abortion statute, Murray's criteria of public order and consent will both discipline and illuminate the debate in church and society."[37] In this, as in any context, civil law must recognize the essentially *moral* nature of law and simultaneously respect the *limited* capacity of the human law to coerce behavior that is in accord with what is right by nature.

Whether the issue at hand is abortion, the question of war and peace, economic equity, or American policy regarding Central America, Hehir accepts the wisdom of Murray's observation that "both the empirical complexity of political issues and the pluralist nature of American polity demand . . . a mode of discourse rooted in a religious vision but expressed in concepts and categories open to rational examination by people of various religious convictions." Without attempting to claim a special role in the preservation and promotion of Murray's method of political and theological reasoning, Hehir recognizes in this method a resource equal to the task of engaging all elements of society "in a serious critique of both [the] substance and style" of the public consensus.[38]

Not all who would preserve and promote Murray's method of political reasoning would join in the adulation of Hehir's effort to appropriate that wisdom in his attempt to offer solutions to the social problems which exist in our contemporary American political milieu. With respect to some of Hehir's conclusions regarding the relationship of religion and politics, one critic, *George Weigel*, argues that his [Hehir's] "thought and work have been the crucial vessel through which the abandonment of the [Catholic] heritage was completed." Weigel argues that Hehir does not share "Murray's views on the problem of communism. . . . His thought on nuclear weapons also involves a kind of determinism which Murray would have rejected, . . . [and he] breaks most decisively with the Murray legacy on the question of America . . . [and] the moral importance of the American experiment in democratic pluralism."[39] It is not my intention to engage in a polemical defense either of Hehir's interpretation of Murray or of Weigel's critique of Hehir. I point out this criticism only to indicate the presence of conflict which necessarily accompanies the emergence of insight into the ramifications and authenticity of applications of the social-ethical imperatives whose outlines Murray traced in order that future generations might bring them to fulfillment.[40]

In his attempt to preserve and promote Murray's legacy, Weigel has focussed almost exclusively on Murray's understanding of the nature of human freedom and the moral imperatives which are derived from this freedom. Weigel canonizes Murray as the leader of the Catholic human rights revolution and considers Murray's accomplishments to lie principally in his statement of the normative value of religious liberty, his arguments regarding the rights of religious persons and groups to engage in public policy debates in the United States, and his contribution to an understanding of "the large-scale question of the structure of freedom in the world."[41]

Weigel believes that Murray's defense of the normative value of religious liberty "clearly established as Catholic doctrine that there [is], within every person, a privileged sanctuary into which state power ought not to tread." His work also committed the Church to "active advocacy on behalf of religious freedom."[42] Finally, Murray's efforts committed the Church to the full patronage of the entire complex of human rights, not simply to the right to religious liberty.

In treating Murray's argument for Catholicism's engagement in American public discourse, Weigel lauds his distinction of society and state, his statement that government is only legitimate when it is established with the consent of the governed, his concept of the necessity of a virtuous citizenry, and his affirmation of the dignity of the human persons to whom human rights adhere both by their very nature and antecedent to their status as citizens.[43] Weigel also credits Murray's defense of the entire matrix of human rights as the inspiration for the universal Catholic commitment to these rights. Murray is thus considered the "herald" of a "human rights revolution"—in Iberia, Poland, in the Philippines, and throughout Central and South America—which has been "more than a rhetorical revolution; it has been a revolution in *praxis* as well."[44]

His contemporaries have criticized Weigel for being too polemical and insensitive to "the complex understanding of rights beyond simple immunities and entitlements."[45] One critic has gone so far as to say that Weigel's works sometimes resemble more a "treatise on the politics of ethics and theology than a treatise on the ethics and theology of politics."[46]

It is true that Weigel sometimes appears to "claim the mantle of Murray" without reflecting the total complexity of Murray's thought. One must judge positively the addition of Weigel's voice to the dialogue, however, for it is only through the interchange of diverse perspectives that the complex dialectical project of fostering the emergence of insight can progress.

There are thus many interpreters of John Courtney Murray's political-theological project. Each makes a unique contribution to an enhanced understanding of the task which faces American Catholics who intend to make a contribution to the public life of this society in a manner that is reflective of their own faith commitment. I have not attempted to pass definitive judgement on the validity of any of these interpretations in order to demonstrate the need to listen to all of the voices present in the contemporary debate regarding the best manner of preserving John Courtney Murray's work as a resource for the continuing effort to promote the actualization of human potentialities in their natural and supernatural dimensions. By examining the strengths and weaknesses of each interpretation, one promotes an inclusive conversation among all who sincerely search for a Truth that is itself liberating. It would be fundamentally inconsistent with Murray's entire intellectual endeavor to bestow a title of exclusive competence on only one of his interpreters, for his was an effort to consider as many diverse and conflicting experiences and understandings as possible before attempting to make judgements and decisions regarding what is ultimately true.

Appendix B

A Final Note on Reinhold Niebuhr's Contribution to Christian Political Theology

ONE SIGNIFICANT LIABILITY WHICH ONE MIGHT ATTRIBUTE TO Murray's description of the principles of Christian constitutionalism is his nearly exclusive recourse to the Thomistic philosophical-theological tradition. While it is no doubt true that the Church has recognized the unique contribution of Thomism to the attempt to understand the mysteries of faith, it is also possible to construct a Christian political theology whose estimation of the possibility of promoting justice and peace is far different from that which Murray derived from Aquinas. One may locate an example of such an alternative Christian political theology in the works of Murray's contemporary, Reinhold Niebuhr.

Niebuhr's Christian political theology bears witness to the trans-temporal wisdom of the fourth century philosopher-theologian, Augustine of Hippo. In contrast to Murray's appropriation of Thomistic principles which yield an optimistic vision of the purpose of politics, Niebuhr's appropriation of Augustinian political theology represents a statement of what has come to be known as "Christian realism." In contrast to Murray's Thomistic assumption that there is "an order in history, conforming to the uniformities of nature," one may locate in Niebuhr's works the Augustinian notion that all human persons possess "the transcendent freedom . . . to defy any rational system." Niebuhr was mystified when he considered the degree to which this

Augustinian insight "into human nature and history . . . [was] subordinated to classical thought . . . in the formulations of Thomas Aquinas." He was likewise adamant in his insistence that there ought to be "more debate between Augustinian and Thomistic" perspectives as Christians continue to investigate the relationship between religion and politics.[1]

As a Christian philosopher-theologian, Niebuhr provided the Augustinian perspective which was necessary lest the wisdom of this tradition become lost in the midst of Murray's Thomism. Like Murray, Niebuhr recognized that "the force of reason makes for justice . . . by placing inner restraints upon the desires of the self . . . [and] by judging the claims and assertions of individuals from the intelligence of the total community." His estimation of the possibility of establishing justice in the temporal society differed from Murray's, however, because he questioned whether "reason is sufficiently powerful to achieve, or even to approximate, a complete harmony and consistency between what is demanded for the self and what is granted to the other."[2] It is quite conceivable that Niebuhr would have judged Murray to have been among those who "are virtuous because they have some conception of a higher law than their own will," but who are also somewhat "foolish because they do not know the power of self-will."[3]

This recognition of the radical freedom of the human will was integral to Niebuhr's understanding of the economy of salvation and to his estimation of the possibility of attaining justice and peace in the temporal world. He proposed that "the essence of man is his freedom," and the sin which obstructs the realization of justice and peace "is committed in that freedom." He insisted that "sin can . . . not be attributed to a defect in . . . [the] essence" of human persons, but it can "be understood as a self-contradiction, made possible by the fact of . . . freedom." All sin, especially the human community's failure to achieve justice and peace, is very serious because it issues from "the very center of the human personality: in the will."[4]

Murray and Niebuhr agreed that the final end of all human persons is the salvation promised by God. Niebuhr's Augustinian perspective, however, provides the basis for an alternative political theology which is at once authentically Christian and legitimately critical of the thoroughly rational perspective of Murray's Thomism. Where

Murray expressed his confidence in the ability of human reason to promote the realization of the immanent common good of the temporal society, Niebuhr would insist that human society itself is responsible for any and all evil present in the world. Any true conversion to justice and peace, he claimed, "would have to come through the intervention of God, [for] the moral resources of men would not be sufficient to guarantee it."[5]

Niebuhr's insights into the nature of the human person and the difficulty of promoting justice and peace in an essentially "immoral society" do not dismantle the philosophical-theological edifice upon which Murray constructed his own political theology. They do, however, constructively indicate that Murray may have failed to appreciate fully the debilitating effects of original sin on those who would attempt to realize the immanent *telos* of the temporal society. Anyone who would attempt to implement the principles of Christian constitutionalism in the twentieth century must therefore also consider the wisdom of Niebuhr's contribution to this political theological project.

Endnotes

Introduction

1. At this point, I will define the "state" simply as that structure within society whose limited concern is the maintenance of public order. [Cf. Richard P. McBrien, *Caesar's Coin: Religion and Politics in America* (New York: Macmillan Publishing Co., 1987), 25, 204.] I will further define the concept of the "state" and its relation to the other orders which compose the greater entity, "society," in my discussion of Murray's differentiation of these concepts in Chapter 2 below.

2. The Second Vatican Council met in four sessions from 1962 through 1965. The best account of the trials and tribulations which beset Murray as a result of the controversial nature of his writings on the Church-state question is to be found in Chapter 2 ("Opposition and Rebuke: 1950-1959") of Donald E. Pelotte, *John Courtney Murray: Theologian in Conflict* (New York: Paulist Press, 1975), 27-73. Pelotte describes Murray's vindication in Chapter 3 ("Vindication: 1960-1967"), 74-114.

Chapter 1

1. John Courtney Murray, S.J., "The Problem of State Religion," *Theological Studies (TS)* 12 (June 1951): 157.

2. This statement appears in Leo XII's encyclical *Nobilissima Gallorum Gens* (1884) and is quoted in Murray, "Leo XIII: Separation of Church and State," *TS* 14 (June 1953): 193.

3. This is Murray's translation of the passage from the twelfth letter of Gelasius which reads: "*Duo quippe sunt, imperator august, quibus principaliter hic mundus regitur: auctoritas sacrata pontificium et regalis potestas. In quibus tanto gravius est pondus sacerdotium.*" A more literal interpretation of "*principaliter*" would indicate that Gelasius intended

to communicate the idea that the royal power may indeed claim some measure of "original" jurisdiction over the citizen. Similarly, a more literal translation renders "*regitur*" as "ruled" rather than "raised." Murray's translation is found in the inaugural lecture in the series, "The Problem of Church and State: Some Perspectives," delivered at Yale University, New Haven, Connecticut, February 2, 1952.

4. Ibid.

5. Ibid.

6. I have drawn heavily from the discussion of this controversy in Volume IV, Part III, Chapters 1-3 in Robert and A.J. Carlyle, *A History of Medieval Political Theory in the West* (New York: Barnes & Noble, Inc., 1903-36). In *The Search for an American Public Theology: The Contribution of John Courtney Murray* (New York: Paulist Press, 1989), 187, n. 31, Robert W. McElroy asserts that Murray himself relied heavily on this work in his analysis of the applications of the Gelasian Thesis.

7. Murray, "The Medieval Situation: One Society, Two Swords," Lecture delivered at Yale University, New Haven, Connecticut, February 5, 1952.

8. Again I rely heavily on Robert and A.J. Carlyle's *History*. Their discussion of the controversy between Boniface VIII and Philip the Fair may be found in *op. cit.*, Volume V, Part II, Chapters 8-10.

9. In both his February 5, 1952 lecture at Yale and in n. 2 in his article "The Problem of State Religion" (cf. n. 1 above), Murray noted that as early as 829 A.D. the Synod of Paris began the practice of substituting the term "*ecclesia*" for the term "hic mundus" in the famous Gelasian text which begins "*Duo sunt . . .*" The implication clearly is, as Murray noted, that "the two societies of earlier times gave way to the one society, 'the Church,' within which the two powers were enclosed, distinct only as functions of the one *corpus christianum*." ("The Problem of State Religion," 155, n.2.)

10. Robert and A.J. Carlyle, *History*, Vol. V, 392. The text of *Unam Sanctam* reads as follows: "In hac ejusque [i.e., the Pope's] potestate duos esse gladios, spiritualem videlicet et temporalem, Evangelicis dictis instruimur. . . . Uterque ergo in potestate ecclesiae spiritualis scilicet gladius et materialis, sed is quidem pro ecclesia, ille vero ab ecclesia exercendus, ille sacerdotis, in manu regum et militum, sed ad nutum et patientiam sacerdotis. Oportet autem gladium esse sub gladio, et temporalem auctoritatem spirituali subjici potestati."

It is of paramount importance to note the juxtaposition of the terms "*auctoritas*" and "*potestas*" in this Bull. Where Gelasius referred to "*auc-*

toritas sacrata pontificium et regalis potestas," Boniface referred to *"temporalem auctoritatem"* and *"spirituali . . . potestati."* According to Murray, "auctoritas" "leads by virtue of its own dignity, and one follows it out of conviction" whereas *"potestas"* "drives by virtue of force and one moves before it in consequence of coercion." Therefore, Boniface appears to have fundamentally inverted the authentic moral bases upon which both the spiritual and the temporal orders may require the assent and compliance of the will of the individual citizen. Cf. n. 3 above and Murray, Yale University Lecture, February 2, 1952.

11. Yale University Lecture, February 5, 1952.

12. Murray began his study of the nature of the two societies by defining the term "society" as "a structured order of human relationships (familial, civic, economic, religious, etc.) which is constituted in view of an end." He further stated that "a society is not constituted by a mass of individuals but by a patterned ensemble of purposive human associations." A society is therefore a form of structured social action—a *conspiratio*—essentially teleological in its character. (Murray, "The Problem of State Religion," 175.)

13. *"Spiritualis immediate [est] a Deo."* Quoted in Murray, "Contemporary Orientations of Catholic Thought on Church and State in the Light of History," TS 10 (June 1949): 203.

14. Quoted in Murray, "Contemporary Orientations," 202, 203. Murray studied John of Paris, *Tractatus de Potestate Regia et Papali* as it was reprinted in Jean Leclercq, *Jean de Paris et l'ecclesiologie du XIIIe siecle* (Paris: Librairie Philosophique J. Vrin, 1942). These quotations may be found at 178 and 207-208. All subsequent references to John's *Tractatus* will include an indication of their location in Murray's article as well as in Leclercq's text.

15. Murray, "Contemporary Orientations," 203-204; Leclercq, 208. Note John's use of the term *potestas* to describe the basis for moral suasion in the means employed by the Church to achieve its end. Though perhaps more faithful than Boniface to the principles of the Gelasian Thesis, his theory nevertheless remains somewhat imperfect as an application of the principles of social dualism. Cf. n. 10 above.

16. *"Homo . . . ordinatur ad finem supernaturalem qui est vita eterna."* Murray, "Contemporary Orientations," 202; Leclercq, 178.

17. *"Homo sit animal naturaliter politicum seu civile ut dicitur I Politicorum."* Murray, "Contemporary Orientations," 198; Leclercq, 177.

18. "*Est . . . tale regimen a iure naturali et a iure gentium derivatum.*" Murray, "Contemporary Orientations," 199; Leclercq, 176-177.

19. "*Ex naturali instinctu qui ex Deo est . . . civiliter et in communitate civitate vivant.*" Murray, "Contemporary Orientations," 199; Leclercq, 180.

20. "*Potestam habet distinctam et sibi propriam quam non habet a papa sed acciperit a Deo immediate.*" Murray, "Contemporary Orientations," 199; Leclercq, 180. The reference to Boniface is mine.

21. "*Iustitia animata et custos iusti.*" Murray, "Contemporary Orientations," 200; Leclercq, 225.

22. Murray, "Contemporary Orientations," 200.

23. See Leclercq, 242.

24. "*Homo . . . ordinatur ad bonum tale quod per naturam acquiri potest, quod est vivere secundum virtutem.*" Murray, "Contemporary Orientations," 199; Leclercq, 178.

25. "*Habet in se rationem boni et appetibilis secundum se cuiusmodi est.*" Murray, "Contemporary Orientations," 199; Leclercq, 227.

26. Quoted in Murray, "Contemporary Orientations," 205. See Leclercq, 212.

27. Murray, "Contemporary Orientations," 205.

28. Murray, "Contemporary Orientations," 43; See also Leclercq, 218.

29. Murray, "Contemporary Orientations," 205.

30. Murray, "The Problem of State Religion," 157, n. 4.

31. Murray, "Contemporary Orientations," 195.

32. Ibid., 204-205.

Chapter 2

1. Oliver Wendell Holmes, Jr., *The Common Law* (Boston: Little, Brown, and Co., 1881), 1.

2. Murray, "Governmental Repression of Heresy," *Proceedings* of the Third Annual Convention of the Catholic Theological Society of America (1948): 26-98; "St. Robert Bellarmine on the Indirect Power," *TS* 9 (December 1948): 491-535.

3. Robert Bellarmine, *De Potestate Summi Pontificis in rebus temporalibus*, III (Opera Omnia [Neapoli, 1856], IV [Pars 2], 270) in "St. Robert Bellarmine," 491.

4. Murray, "St. Robert Bellarmine," 491-492.

5. Ibid., 492. Murray also stated that "in its own setting it was a splendid piece of theological argument. But it is no derogation of Bellarmine's

greatness to say that as a theory, it was transitional." ("Governmental Repression of Heresy," 43.)

6. Bellarmine, *De S. Pont.*, V, 1, 524 in "St. Robert Bellarmine," 496. In Bellarmine's own words: "*(Intelligimus) potestatem pontificium per se et propie spiritualem esse, et ideo directe respicere, ut objectum suum principarium, spiritualia negotia; sed indirecte respicere, idest, per ordinem ad spiritualia, reductive, et per necessariam consequentiam, ut sic loquamur, respicere temporalia, ut objectum secundarium, ad quod non convertitur haec potestas spiritualis nisi in casu.*" Quoted in "Governmental Repression of Heresy," 44.

7. For example, note Bellarmine's continued use of the phrase "*potestatem pontificium*" in n. 6 above. In practice, if not in theory, Bellarmine's political theology appears to resemble Boniface's theory of the "Two Swords" much more closely than it does Gelasius' theory of the "Two Societies."

8. Bellarmine, *De S. Pont.*, V, 6, 532 in "St. Robert Bellarmine," 498.

9. Murray, "St. Robert Bellarmine," 499-501. See also "Governmental Repression of Heresy," 45.

10. Murray argued that while the premises of Bellarmine's theory "are different from those of the theory of the direct power, . . . in their essential conclusions the two theories present differences that are more apparent than real." ("Governmental Repression of Heresy," 45.)

11. "St. Robert Bellarmine," 502. Murray noted that in arguing from principles to conclusions in justifying his own conception of a practical relationship between Church and state in the *respublica christiana*, it was often necessary for Bellarmine to "appeal to the factual and juridical peculiarities of a special historical situation, which are contingent." To the degree to which practice informed Bellarmine's theory, it also diminished its status as a transtemporal statement of Catholic Church-state theory. See "Governmental Repression of Heresy," 49.

12. Even as great a thinker as Aquinas reflected the immaturity of the political philosophy of that period. For example, though he appreciated the inherent dignity and autonomy of the temporal power, Aquinas may have misrepresented the true nature of the temporal society when he wrote that "kings are vassals of the Church" without explaining the nuanced use of that phrase in a manner that reflected the traditional principles of social dualism.

13. "St. Robert Bellarmine," 503-504.

14. Bellarmine developed his political theology while he was engaged in po-
    lemical struggles against: 1) the "Seven Fools of Venice" regarding the
    privileges of the clergy *vis à vis* the state; 2) James I of England and his
    notion of royal absolutism; and 3) the theorists promoting absolutism—
    e.g., William Barclay and Roger Widdrington.

15. "St. Robert Bellarmine," 527, 528, 532.

16. Murray expressed his appreciation of the complexity of Bellarmine's theo-
    logical project when he wrote that it was to Bellarmine's credit that he
    was able to explain the "spiritual character of the Church's power against
    the 'temporalization' of it by the direct-power theory" while simulta-
    neously insisting that "the spiritual power of the Church has a real reach
    into the temporal order of society" ("Governmental Repression of
    Heresy," 44).

17. "St. Robert Bellarmine," 533.

18. Ibid., 504-505.

19. Ibid., 518.

20. Leo's pontificate spanned the years 1878-1903. His major Gelasian texts,
    according to Murray, included: *Arcanum* (1880), *Nobilissima Gallorum
    Gens* (1884), *Immortale Dei* (1885), *Officio Sanctissimo* (1887),
    Sapientiae Christianae (1890), *Praeclara Gratulationis* (1894), and
    Parvenuti (1902). Murray summarized these texts in "Leo XIII: Separa-
    tion of Church and State," 192-200.

    It is interesting to note that Murray never explicilty included the letter
    Longinqua Oceani (1895) in any listing of the major Leonine texts which
    addressed the Church-state question. Reasons for such an omission as-
    suredly include his desire to maintain the independence of his own en-
    deavors from efforts to promote an "Americanist" agenda as well as his
    conviction that the issues he was investigating were not confined to the
    American milieu but rather universal in their scope.

21. Quoted in Murray, "Leo XIII: Separation of Church and State," 194.

22. Ibid.

23. Ibid., 194-195.

24. Ibid., 194.

25. See Murray's analysis of these texts in ibid., 192-199.

26. Quoted in ibid., 194, 196, 198.

27. Ibid., 196.

28. Ibid., 193.

29. Ibid., 194, 197, 199.

30. Ibid., 194, 197.

31. See ibid., 192-199, *passim.*

32. Quoted in ibid., 193, 197.

33. Ibid., 209.

34. Ibid., 213.

35. Among the difficulties immediately evident in this articulation of Catholic doctrine is its apparent assumption that the Church *directly* has a power to influence the affairs of the temporal society. This statement also seems to envision a "paternalistic" concept of the state (a topic which we will consider shortly). Finally, to anticipate the direction which Murray's investigation would later take, this teaching also seems to ignore the strictly "juridic" nature of the power of the state, and it implies a competency for the state in promoting matters religious which the Fathers of the Second Vatican Council would eventually deny.

36. Murray, "The Problem of State Religion," 158, n. 6.

37. McBrien, *op. cit.,* 25. The *principle of subsidiarity,* first articulated in a magisterial statement by Pius XI in *Quadragesimo Anno* (1931), insists that the natural autonomy of these various insititutions within civil society must be protected and preserved from interference by larger institutions, including, and especially, the state: "it is an injustice and at the same time a grave evil and disturbance of right order to assign to a greater and higher association what lesser and subordinate organizations can do" (*QA* 79).

38. The efforts of religious organizations to provide such benefits as education, health care, and housing are but a few obvious examples of the manner in which the institutions of the spiritual society contribute to the realization of the common good in the secular society without assuming the direct promotion of such temporal goods as one of its principle functions.

39. Murray, "The Problem of State Religion," 158, n. 6.

40. Ibid.

41. It is in this definition of the nature of the state that Murray made the distinction between society and state which was truly the cornerstone not only of his critique of existing Church-state theory but also of his positive construction of the appropriate relationship between religion and politics. Both Murray and Leo XIII insisted that the state's "functions are not coextensive with the functions of society; they are limited by the fact that it is only one, though the highest, subsidiary function of society." (Ibid.)

42. Ibid., 158-159, n. 6.

43. Quoted in Murray, "Leo XIII: Separation of Church and State," 197.

44. Ibid., 194.

45. Ibid., 195-196.

46. Ibid., 196.

47. Murray, "Leo XIII on Church and State: The Structure of the Controversy," *TS* 14 (March 1953): 1-30.

48. "Leo XIII: Separation of Church and State," esp. 145-187.

49. See Leo XIII, *Gratiam Scito* (1889) in *Leonis Papae XIII Allocutiones, Epistolae, Constitutiones*, 7 vols. (Paris: Desclee, 1887-), III, 232; also: *Quod Nuper*, in *Acta Sanctae Sedis* (*ASS*), (1888-9), 706; and *Parvenuti, ASS*, XXXIV (1901-2), 526-527.

50. Murray, "Leo XIII on Church and State: The General Structure of the Controversy," 11.

51. Murray, "Leo XIII: Separation of Church and State," 145.

52. See *Praeclara Gratulationis* (1894), in *Lettres Apostoliques de Leon XIII, Encycliques, Brefs, etc., Texte latin avec traduction francaise*, 7 vols. (Paris: Maison de la Bonne Presse), IV, 96-98.

53. See, in addition to those listed in n. 20 above, *Inscrutabili* (1878), *Quod Apostolici Muneris* (1878), *Diuturnum* (1881), *Etsi Nos* (1882), *Humanum Gens* (1884), *Jampridem Nobis* (1886), *Quantunque Le Siano* (1887), *Libertas* (1888), *E Giunto* (1889), *Dall'alto* (1890), *Rerum Novarum* (1891), *Au milieu* (1892), *Inimica Vis* (1892), *Gardien de cette foi* (1892), and *Graves de commune* (1901).

54. *Immortale Dei* (1885), Desclee, II, 157-158.

55. J.L. Talmon, *The Rise of Totalitarian Democracy* (Boston: Beacon Press, 1952).

56. *Immortale Dei*, Desclee, II, 157-158.

57. Murray, "Leo XIII: Separation of Church and State," 159.

58. Murray, "Leo XIII: Two Concepts of Government," *TS* 14 (December 1953): 551.

59. *Rerum Novarum* (1891), quoted in ibid., 552-553.

60. Ibid., 559.

61. Ibid., 559-560.

62. Ibid., 555, 556.

63. Murray, "Leo XIII: Two Concepts of Government: Government and the Order of Culture," *TS* 15 (March 1954): 4, 7, 12-13.

64. Ibid., 15, 17, 18.

65. Ibid., 28.

66. Murray explained this element of Leo's political theology in an article which he was never allowed to publish because of the objections of those in the Roman curia who viewed his work as a departure from the Church's teaching as it was being articulated in the twentieth century. ["Leo XIII and Pius XII: Government and the Order of Religion."] Donald Pelotte describes the events surrounding the censorship of this article in *op. cit.*, 51-54. The article will be published in a forthcoming volume edited by J. Leon Hooper, S.J.—over thirty-five years after it was originally written!

67. Leo XIII, *Immortale Dei*, quoted in "Leo XIII and Pius XII: Government and the Order of Religion," Galley 13. [The galley sheets for this unpublished article are located in the Archives of the Woodstock College Library, Georgetown University, Washington, DC.]

68. Murray, "Leo XIII and Pius XII: Government and the Order of Religion," Galley 13.

69. The "Leonine Series" is said to include the following articles: "The Church and Totalitarian Democracy," *TS* 13 (December 1952): 525-63; "Leo XIII on Church and State: The General Structure of the Controversy;" "Leo XIII: Separation of Church and State;" "Leo XIII: Two Concepts of Government;" "Leo XIII: Two Concepts of Government: Government and the Order of Culture;" and "Leo XIII and Pius XII: Government and the Order of Religion."

Although he acknowledged his role as that of the critic, Murray also attempted to alleviate the fears of those who questioned his orthodoxy when he wrote that "it is no derogation of the authority of Leo XIII's encyclicals to say that they were, rather importantly, tracts for the times." ("Leo XIII and Pius XII: Government and the Order of Religion," Galley 13.)

In fact, it is not truly accurate to label Murray a "critic" of Leo's political theology. It is no doubt true that he approached Leo's writings from the perspective of a professional theologian. However, Murray actually defended Leo's articulation of the *principles* of social dualism. It seems that he found most distressing the misapplication of Leo's political theology by his contemporaries in the twentieth century.

70. See Thomas Aquinas, *Summa Theologica*, Ia, IIae, QQ. 90-94.

71. Murray, "Leo XIII and Pius XII: Government and the Order of Religion," Galley 13.

72. Ibid., Galley 22.

73. Ibid., Galley 19.

Chapter 3

1. *John Courtney Murray: Contemporary Church-State Theory* (Garden City, NY: Doubleday & Co., Inc., 1965).

2. Ibid., 29. Indicative of this position is Ryan's statement that "the State must . . . recognize the *true* religion. This means the form of religion professed by the Catholic Church." Further, "the State should officially recognize the Catholic religion as the religion of the commonwealth" because "the public profession, protection, and promotion of this religion, and the legal prohibition of all direct assaults upon it . . . [is] one of the most obvious and fundamental duties of the State." From: John A. Ryan and Francis J. Boland, *Catholic Principles of Politics* (New York: The Macmillan Company, 1940), 313-314, 316, 319. [These and all references to Ryan's work in the notes that follow are quotations from his commentary on *Immortale Dei* which originally appeared in Ryan and F.X. Millar, *The State and the Church* (New York: Macmillan Co., 1922). Thus, these references are to work completed by 1922.] Cf. George W. Shea, "Catholic Doctrine and 'The Religion of the State,'" *The American Ecclesiastical Review* (*AER*) 123 (September 1950): 166, 167, 173, 174; Francis J. Connell, "Christ the King of Civil Rulers," *AER* 119 (October 1948): 244-253; Joseph Clifford Fenton, "The Theology of the Church and the State," *Proceedings* of the Second Annual Meeting of the Catholic Theological Society of America, Boston, 1947, 32, 33, 40, and "Principles Underlying Traditional Church-State Doctrine," *AER* 126 (June 1952): 457; and Alfredo Cardinal Ottaviani, "Church and State: Some Present Problems in Light of the Teachings of Pope Pius XII," *AER* 128 (May 1953): 322, 325. Murray himself wrote in 1945 that "the State has the obligation to acknowledge God as its author, to worship Him as He wills to be worshipped, and to subject its official life and action to His law" (Freedom of Religion: I. The Ethical Problem," *TS* 6 (June 1945): 241-242). However, shortly after the publication of this article, he recognized the inadequacy of this "traditional" view of Church-state relations. He then began the process of re-evaluating the ethical imperatives which followed from a profession of the truth of the Catholic faith, particularly with regard to the issues of establishment and toleration. The reasons for his abandonment of this traditional view and his subsequent defense of the normative value of the principle of religious liberty will be addressed below.

3. Ibid. Fenton was crystal clear on the first portion of this assertion in "The Teachings of *Ci riesce*," *AER* 130 (February 1954) when he wrote that "that which is not in accord with truth or with the standard of morality has, objectively, no right to exist, no right to be taught, no right to be done," and therefore there could be "no objections raised against the teaching or the terminology of writers who hold that . . . error has no rights" (116, 122). On the need to balance a respect for the individual's *private* right to freedom of conscience against the state's duty to repress heresy, Shea wrote that "it is agreed to by all that the members of sects must be permitted the private external exercise of their religion." However, in a state in which Catholics are in the majority, the government would "be under moral obligation . . . to restrict sects in such matters as the public profession and exercise of their false religion, in their propaganda, [and] the spread of their heretical doctrines" (*op. cit.*, 168). Cf. Ryan and Boland, *op. cit.*, 314, 317-318; Connell, *op. cit.*, 250, and "The Theory of the 'Lay State,'" *AER* 125 (July 1951): 17; and Ottaviani, *op. cit.*, 328.

4. The very concept of "the religion of the state" proved to be one of the most tendentious elements of the dispute between Murray and his antagonists. Ryan, *et al.*, held that it is an obvious element of Catholic doctrine that "the state should officially recognize the Catholic religion as the religion of the commonwealth . . . [in] a political community that is either exclusively, or almost exclusively, made up of Catholics" (*op. cit.*, 316, 319). According to Murray, however, Catholic doctrine insists, not on the need to secure the establishment of the Catholic Church as "the religion of the state," but on the normative value of the freedom of the Church. So long as Catholics enjoy the liberty to profess their faith and publicly worship as a community, "the dogmatic concept of 'the freedom of the Church' . . . [does not] entail by necessary consequence the constitutional concept, 'the religion of the state.'" ["Current Theology: On Religious Freedom," *TS* 10 (June 1949): 422.]

5. These are the essential principles of the so-called Catholic *thesis* and *hypothesis*. (Love, *op. cit.*, 29-30.) Shea was the most clear on the distinction between the *thesis* and the *hypothesis*. He described the Church's "official" teaching as follows: 1) "In a Catholic society, it is incumbent upon the State to be a 'Catholic State.' The formal, official, and exclusive recognition and profession of Catholicism by the State in a Catholic society as its own one and only religion, in short, the establishment of Catholicism as the 'religion of the state,' seems necessarily contained in the very notion of the state's duty to profess the true religion, therefore, Catholi-

cism, with its creed, code, [and] cult." (*op. cit.*, 167-168.) 2) "State toleration of non-Catholic denominations is justifiable only under certain circumstances, in order to avoid a greater evil or to preserve some greater
good; in decreeing toleration under such circumstances, the state may go
only as far as the common good requires." ["Spain and Religious Freedom," *AER* 127 (September 1952): 169. Cf. Ryan and Boland, *op. cit.*,
320; Connell, "Reply to Father Murray," *AER* 126 (February 1952): 57;
Fenton, "Principles Underlying Traditional Church-State Doctrine," 459,
461, "Teachings of *Ci riesce*," 120; and Ottaviani, *op. cit.*, 325, and *Institutiones Iuris Publici Ecclesiastici* (Rome: Typis Polyglottis Vaticanis,
1936), vol. II, 71.]

6. Ibid., 30. Ryan wrote that "while all this is very true in logic and in theory, the event of its practical realization in any state or country is so remote in time and in probability that no practical man will let it disturb his
equanimity or affect his attitude toward those who differ from him in religious faith" (*op. cit.*, 320).

I would tend to dispute Love's claim that this fourth element may be
considered integral to the position of Murray's contemporaries (especially
since many prominent theologians steadfastly maintained the legitimacy of
the *thesis/hypothesis* distinction). For example, Connell wrote that although "the traditional idea of the relation between Church and state constitutes no menace to the cherished spirit of liberty so dear to all our
citizens," nevertheless, the Church will not tolerate any "compromise of
the principle that Jesus Christ established a Church to which he gave special rights and immunities, to the end that it might bring all men the message of the Gospel and the means of attaining life eternal" [*Freedom of
Worship: The Catholic Position* (New York: Paulist Press, 1944), 18].
Fenton affirmed this sentiment in 1954 when he wrote that as a result of
Pius XII's allocution *Ci riesce*, the perpetual "legitimacy of the explanation of the relationship between Church and state in terms of *thesis* and
hypothesis will be acknowledged" ("Teachings of *Ci riesce*," 123).

7. Father Hooper has given a full analysis of these eight stages in the development of Murray's theory of religious liberty in Chapters 1, 2, and 4 of *The
Ethics of Discourse: The Social Philosophy of John Courtney Murray*
(Washington, DC: Georgetown University Press, 1986), 30-81, 121-156.
He has also provided a detailed outline and bibliography of Murray's
works published during these eight stages in an Introduction to a chapter
on religious liberty in a forthcoming volume of Murray's writings which
he is editing. I am grateful to Father Hooper for making this Introduction

available to me and for his insights into the development of Murray's thought.

8. The term "manualist" refers to the method of moral reasoning employed in the manuals of moral theology which were standard textbooks used by seminary educators. The defects inherent in this method are discussed below.

9. Murray, "Current Theology: Freedom of Religion," *TS* 6 (March 1945): 87.

10. Murray, "Freedom of Religion I: The Ethical Problem," 241.

11. Ibid., 239-240.

12. Ibid., 241-242.

13. Ibid., 242, 243, 254. To avoid any appearance of ethical relativism, Murray duly noted that "conscience is not the norm of its own rightness; it is itself regulated by a higher norm, not of its own creation—the eternal law of God." (Ibid., 245.)

14. Ibid., 263.

15. Ibid., 263-264.

16. Here defined as an "organized society with its agencies of government." (Ibid.)

17. Ibid.

18. Ibid.

19. Ibid., 266-267.

20. Love, *op. cit.*, 48.

21. Ibid., 48. One may find the outline of Murray's theological and political arguments which were to follow the publication of this ethical argument in a memorandum which he had prepared for Archbishop Edward Mooney in April, 1945. (Murray Archives, file 326.) Fr. Hooper has analyzed these arguments and accounted for their failure in *op. cit.*, 30-50.

22. See Hooper, *op. cit.*, 45-46.

23. See Ibid., 46-47.

24. For a more detailed explanation of these criticisms of Murray's first attempt to defend the principle of religious liberty, see ibid., 47-49.

25. Love, *op. cit.*, 48.

26. "Governmental Repression of Heresy," 33.

27. *Summa Theologica*, I-II, Q. 94 art. 5; Q. 97, art. 1.

28. "Contemporary Orientations," 220. See also *Summa Theologica*, I-II, Q. 95, art. 2: "every human law has just so much the nature of law as it is derived from the law of nature."

29. "Governmental Repression of Heresy," 63.

30. "Contemporary Orientations," 234.

31. The title of this section refers to the fact that the principal exchanges between Murray and his interlocutors took place in the pages of the *American Ecclesiastical Review* which was published at the Catholic University of America in Washington, DC.

32. See Shea, "Catholic Doctrine and 'The Religion of the State,'" 164-165. This is a reference to Murray, "Freedom of Religion I: The Ethical Problem," 266, fn. 9b.

33. Ibid., 167-168.

34. Murray, "The Problem of 'The Religion of the State,'" *AER* 124 (May 1951): 327-352. Also published as "The Problem of State Religion," *TS* 12 (June 1951): 155-178. My references will be to the *TS* article.

35. See Chapter 2 (above) for Murray's definition of these terms.

36. "The Problem of State Religion," 155-159.

37. Ibid., 160, 161.

38. Ibid., 163. The democratic tradition Murray described here was of course that of the Anglo-Saxon variety. He continued to characterize the continental liberal tradition as secularist in origin and totalitarian in its ultimate tendency.

39. Ibid., 163, 164.

40. On the origins of the use of this distinction, see Maurice Benevot, "Thesis and Hypothesis," *TS* 15 (September 1954): 440-446.

41. See Connell, "Christ the King of Civil Rulers," 244-253.

42. Connell, "The Theory of the 'Lay State,'" 11, 17.

43. Ibid., 18.

44. Murray, "For the Freedom and Transcendence of the Church," *AER* 126 (January 1952): 29.

45. "The Problem of State Religion," 175.

46. Ibid., 177.

47. Connell, "Reply to Father Murray," 54.

48. Ibid., 56.

49. Ibid., 57-58.

50. Murray, "Problem of State Religion," 170.

51. Murray, "The Church and Totalitarian Democracy," 525-563.

52. Ibid., 552-553.

53. Murray, "Leo XIII on Church and State: The General Structure of the Controversy," 1-30.

54. Ibid., 10-11.

55. Ibid., 21.

56. "Leo XIII: Separation of Church and State," 148, 149.

57. Ibid., 151-152.

58. Ibid., 174.

59. Ibid., 168.

60. Ibid., 185-188.

61. Ibid., 156.

62. See "Leo XIII: Two Concepts of Government," 551-567, *passim*.

63. See "Leo XIII: Two Concepts of Government: Government and the Order of Culture," 1-33, *passim*; and "Leo XIII and Pius XII: Government and the Order of Religion," *passim*.

64. See Pelotte, *op. cit.*, esp. 44-59, for details of the censorship of Murray's works.

65. Murray, "On the Structure of the Church-State Problem," in Waldemar Gurian and M.A. Fitzsimons, eds., *The Catholic Church in World Affairs* (Notre Dame, IN: University of Notre Dame Press, 1954), 24.

66. Ibid., 24.

67. Ibid., 25.

68. Ibid., 27.

69. Ibid., 31, 32.

70. The text of this address may be found in *AER* 130 (February 1954): 129-138.

71. See especially Fenton, "The Teachings of *Ci riesce*," 114-123; and "Toleration and the Church-State Controversy," *AER* 130 (May 1954): 330-343.

72. Notes to *Ci riesce*, Murray Archives, file 402, 2.

73. Ibid., 2.

74. Ibid., 2-3.

75. Ibid., 5.

76. Ibid., 7-8.

77. Ibid.

78. "Church and State: The Structure of the Argument," 1958, Murray Archives, file 614; and "*Unica Status Religio*," 1959, Murray Archives, file 611. The first of these articles is to be published in the previously mentioned volume to be edited by Hooper.

79. "Church and State: The Structure of the Argument," 1-4.

80. Ibid., 4-6.

81. Ibid., 7-8.

82. Ibid., 8-10.

83. Ibid., 13-14.

84. Ibid., 15.

85. Ibid., 15-17.

86. Ibid., 19.

87. Ibid., 20.

88. Ibid., 21; cf. Aquinas, *Summa Theologica*, I-II, q. 95, art. 1.

89. Ibid., 26-28.

90. Ibid., 29-30.

Chapter 4

1. See Pelotte, *op. cit.*, 77; also, 108-109, n. 28. For a thorough treatment of the Council's activity regarding the Declaration on Religious Liberty, see Gerald P. Fogarty, *The Vatican and the American Hierarchy from 1870 to 1965* (Wilmington, DE: Michael Glazier, Inc., 1985), 386-399 and Pelotte, *op. cit.*, 77-101. For Murray's own description of these events, see "Religious Freedom," in Murray, ed., *Freedom and Man* (New York: P.J. Kenedy and Sons, 1965), 131-140 and "The Declaration on Religious Freedom: A Moment in its Legislative History," in Murray, ed., *Religious Liberty: An End and a Beginning* (New York: The Macmillan Co., 1966), 15-42.

2. The Secretariat's text would have formed part of its schema on ecumenism; the Theological Commission's text, which framed the issue specifically in terms of the Church-state question and also employed the *thesis/hypothesis* distinction, was to have become a chapter in its schema on the Church. (See Fogarty, *op. cit.*, 390.)

3. See Pelotte, *op. cit.*, 81-82.

4. Murray, "On Religious Liberty," *America* 109 (30 November 1963): 705.

5. Ibid., 706.

6. Murray, "The Problem of Religious Freedom," *TS* 25 (December 1964): 503-575. Also published as *The Problem of Religious Freedom*, Woodstock Papers, Number 7 (Westminster, MD: The Newman Press, 1965). My references are to its publication in book form.

7. Ibid., 7, 10, 12.

8. Ibid., 17, 18. Murray pointed to John XXIII's encyclical *Pacem in Terris* (1963) as a clear example of the papal magisterium taking cognizance of modern "man's awareness of his rights." According to Pope John, human persons had become increasingly aware that, by virtue of their inherent human dignity, they possessed the right to enjoy the benefits of the political, economic, and cultural orders of society. Included among these rights which modern man deemed fundamental was, of course, the right "to worship God in accordance with the right dictates of his own conscience, and to profess his religion both in public and in private" (See *Pacem in Terris*, nos. 11-27).

Murray could thus claim papal approbation for his assertion that religious freedom ought to be an integral component of any effort to order the relationship between Church and state.

For Murray's analysis of this encyclical, see "Things Old and New in *Pacem in Terris*," *America* 108 (27 April 1963): 612-614.

9. Ibid., 19.

10. Ibid., 20-22.

11. Ibid., 22-23.

12. Ibid., 25.

13. Ibid., 28-31, 76.

14. "This Matter of Religious Freedom," *America* 112 (9 January 1965): 40-43.

15. Ibid., 42.

16. Ibid., 43.

17. *Dignitatis Humanae*, The Declaration on Religious Liberty, December 7, 1965, no. 3. Quoted in Austin Flannery, ed., *Vatican II: The Conciliar and Post-Conciliar Documents* (Northport, NY: Costello Publishing Co., 1975), 801-802.

18. Ibid., no. 3 in Flannery, 803.

19. Murray, "The Vatican Declaration on Religious Freedom: An Aspect of its Significance," in *The University in the American Experience* (New York: Fordham University, 1966), 2. This speech was also published as "The Declaration on Religious Freedom: Its Deeper Significance," *America* 114 (23 April 1966): 592-593. My references are to the Fordham publication.

20. Ibid., 2, 5-6.

21. Ibid., 9.

22. "The Declaration on Religious Freedom: A Moment in its Legislative History," 38.

23. Ibid., 38-39.

24. Ibid., 39.

25. Ibid., 40-41.

26. Ibid., 41-42.

27. Murray, "The Declaration on Religious Freedom," in John H. Miller, ed., *Vatican II: An Interfaith Appraisal* (Notre Dame, IN: Association Press, 1966), 576.

28. Murray, *We Hold These Truths* (*WHTT*) (Kansas City, MO: Sheed and Ward, 1960), x.

Chapter 5

1. Murray held this position steadfastly throughout all of his published works. Contemporary polticial theorists and theologians, however, are beginning to search for a manner of including the moral wisdom contained in revealed truths in public discourse. (See Appendix below.)

2. Murray relied almost exclusively on Thomas Aquinas' *Treatise on Law* (*Summa Theologica*, I-II, QQ. 90-114) in his description of the natural law tradition.

3. Murray, "How Liberal is Liberalism?" *America* 75 (6 April 1946): 6, 7.

4. Murray, "Reversing the Secularist Drift," *Thought* 24 (March 1949): 37, 38.

5. Ibid., 39.

6. Ibid.

7. Ibid., 39, 40.

8. See *WHTT*, Introduction, 12-14. This Introduction had previously appeared as "America's Four Conspiracies" in John Cogley, ed., *Religion in America* (New York: Meridian Books, 1958), 12-41, and in *The Catholic Mind* 57 (May-June 1959), 230-241.

9. Ibid.

10. See *WHTT*, Chapter 9, "Are There Two or One?" 201-205. This chapter had previously appeared as "The Freedom of Man in the Freedom of the Church," *Modern Age: A Conservative Review* 1 (Fall 1957): 134-145 and in A. Robert Camponigri, ed., *Modern Catholic Thinkers* (New York: Harper, 1960), 372-384 and as "Church, State, and Political Freedom," *The Catholic Mind* 57 (May-June 1959): 216-229.

11. Ibid., 205-211.

12. Ibid., 211-212. This idea is very reminiscent of the thesis which runs through the works of Eric Voegelin and Dante Germino. There is no doubt that Murray was familiar with Voegelin's works; he referred to them in the articles in which he criticized the secularization of society. For a more complete explanation of the thesis that Marxism and communism represent the logical conclusion of political modernity, see Eric Voegelin, *From Enlightenment to Revolution*, ed., John H. Hollowell (Durham, NC: Duke University Press, 1975) and Dante Germino, *Beyond Ideology: The Renewal of Political Theory* (Chicago, IL: The University of Chicago Press, 1967), esp. Chapter 3, 56-66.

13. Ibid., 212.

14. Ibid., 214-215.

15. Ibid., 216.

16. Ibid., 216; "How Liberal is Liberalism?," 7. One may object that theocratic states themselves are the most prone to sectarian violence. This may indeed be true, but theocracy itself is hardly consistent with the principles of social dualism and the tenets of the Gelasian Thesis which are the "religious principles" and "moral purposes" to which Murray referred.

17. Ibid., 217.

18. Murray, "Separation of Church and State," *America* 76 (7 December 1946): 261.

19. Ibid., 262.

20. See Murray, "Religious Liberty: The Concern of All," *America* 77 (7 February 1948): 513-516 for an early statement of his call for ecumenical action to reverse the secularist drift.

21. Murray attempted to "relieve the word 'conspiracy' of its invidious connotations" by referring to its original Latin sense of "unison, concord, unanimity in opinion and feeling, a 'breathing together.'" In this sense, the term "acquires inevitably the connotation of united action for a common end about which there is agreement." This understanding of "conspiracy"

traces its roots to Cicero and the Stoics and retains this meaning through the Scholastic period to the present. (*WHTT*, Introduction, 22.)

22. See *WHTT*, Introduction, 15-22.

23. *WHTT*, Chapter 2, "Civil Unity and Religious Integrity: The Articles of Peace," 45. This chapter, and Chapter 1, "E Pluribus Unum: The American Consensus," had previously appeared as "The Problem of Pluralism in America," in *Thought* 24 (Summer 1954): 165-208; *Catholicism in America* (College of New Rochelle, 1955), 13-38; and *The Catholic Mind* 57 (May-June 1959): 201-215.

24. Ibid., 45.

25. *WHTT*, Chapter 4, "The Origins and Authority of the Public Consensus: A Study of the Growing End," 96, 106-107.

26. Ibid., 109.

27. *WHTT*, Chapter 13, "The Doctrine Lives," 327-328. This chapter had previously appeared as "The Natural Law" in Robert M. MacIver, ed., *Great Expressions of Human Rights* (New York: Harper, 1950), 69-104, and as "Natural Law and the Public Consensus" in John Cogley, ed., *Natural Law and Modern Society* (Cleveland, OH: World Publishing Co., 1962), 48-81.

28. Ibid., 332.

29. Ibid., 333.

30. Ibid., 334. Cf. Chapter 2, n. 37 above.

31. Ibid.

32. Ibid., 114, 115,.

33. Ibid., 115.

34. Murray provided a description of an "elite" which would bear the responsibility for these elements of the public consensus. (See, for example, *WHTT*, 103.) While the problem of positing the existence of an "elite" in American society might undermine the relevance of Murray's "American political theory," his proposition gains some plausibility if one eschews the concept of a social elite and instead recognizes our political officials as the members of society who especially bear the responsibility for this aspect of the public consensus.

35. Ibid., 116.

36. Ibid., 119.

37. Ibid., 121.

38. Murray considered the issue of censorship in its most general terms. He did not address the specific question of determining standards for regulating the use of federal grants for writers and artists—an issue which has recently been the subject of heated debate in our society.

39. *WHTT*, Chapter 7, "Should There Be a Law?," 156. This chapter had previously appeared as "Questions of Striking a Right Balance: Literature and Censorship," *Books on Trial* 14 (June-July 1956): 393-395 and "Literature and Censorship," *The Catholic Mind* 54 (December 1956): 665-677.

40. Ibid., 156.

41. It is important to remember that whenever he employed "rights" language, Murray always assumed that a correlative responsibility adheres to the exercise of such rights—these rights are never absolute as the continental liberal philosophers might have assumed.

42. Ibid., 160, 164.

43. Ibid., 165-166.

44. Ibid., 166. This is especially true in a religiously pluralistic society in which "basic religious divisions lead to a conflict of moral views, certain asserted 'rights' clash with other 'rights' no less strongly asserted, [a]nd the divergences are often irreducible." (Ibid., 167.)

45. Ibid., 169.

46. Ibid., 168.

47. Ibid.

48. Henry J. Abraham, *Freedom and the Court*, 5th ed. (New York: Oxford University Press, 1988), 333. The Court adopted this theory as the norm for adjudicating establishment clause cases in *Everson v. Board of Education*, 330 U.S. 1 (1947) and *McCollum v. Board of Education*, 333 U.S. 203 (1948). For a study of the evolution and demise of this and other norms of establishment clause adjudication, see Abraham, 325-392.

49. See Murray, "The Court Upholds Religious Freedom," *America* 76 (8 March 1947): 628-630. The optimistic title of this article reflects Murray's approval of the *result* of the *Everson* case which held that a "child-benefit" theory allowed a New Jersey statute providing public funds for the transportation of parochial school students to pass constitutional muster. The controlling and dissenting opinions in this case, however, both referred to an absolute wall of separation of Church and state. The use of this absolute standard as the basis for the *McCollum* decision denying the constitutionality of a "released-time" program to allow for the

religious education of children *in* public schools drew Murray's ire and prompted him to attack the reasoning of both decisions in future articles.

50. Murray, "Law or Prepossessions," in Robert G. McCloskey, ed., *Essays in Constitutional Law* (New York: Alfred A. Knopf, 1957), 325, 327-328. This chapter also appeared in *Law and Contemporary Problems* 14 (Winter 1949): 23-43.

51. Ibid., 329, 330-331.

52. Ibid., 332, 335.

53. Murray, "The Court Upholds Religious Freedom," 628.
    There was legal precedent to support Murray's claim that the Justices ought to have considered the school question, not in terms of the "wall" between Church and state, but in terms of the "wall" between state authority and parental conscience. In *Pierce v. Society of Sisters of the Holy Names of Jesus and Mary* [268 U.S. 510 (1925)], the Court ruled unanimously that an Oregon law requiring children to attend public schools interfered "with the liberty of parents and guardians to direct the upbringing and education of children under their control." The Court held that "the child is not the mere creature of the State," nor is there any "general power of the state" to force children "to accept instruction from public teachers only." Rather, the principle agents responsible for the education of children are "those who nurture [them] and direct [their] destiny"—i.e., their parents and guardians.

54. Murray, "Separation of Church and State: True and False Concepts," *America* 76 (15 February 1947): 542, 544.

55. WHTT, Chapter 6, "Is It Justice?" 146. This chapter had previously appeared as "The School Problem in Mid-Twentieth Century" in *The Role of the Independent School in Mid-Twentieth Century America* (Milwaukee, WI: Marquette University Press, 1956), 1-16, and as "The Religious School in a Pluralistic Society," *The Catholic Mind* 54 (September 1956): 143-154.

56. Ibid., 144, 147-148.

57. Ibid., 151.

58. Ibid. See Douglas, writing for the Court in *Zorach v. Clauson*, 343 U.S. 306 (1952) at 313, in a decision that allowed New York schools to continue to permit students to be released from classes in public schools in order to attend religious instruction classes at sites *outside* the public school.

59. Ibid., 153-154.

Chapter 6

1. In an age in which Catholic theologians took great care to avoid the appearance of conflict within the Church, Murray's scholarly integrity was truly admirable—especially when one considers that the objects of his criticism included two canonized saints—Gregory VII and Robert Bellarmine!

2. See Fenton, "The Theology of the Church and the State," "Principles Underlying Traditional Church-State Doctrine," The Teachings of *Ci riesce*," "Toleration and the Church-State Controversy," and "The Holy Father's Statement on Relations between Church and State," *AER* 133 (November 1955): 323-331; also Connell, "Pope Leo XIII's Message to America," *AER* 109 (October 1943): 249-256, "The Theory of the 'Lay State,'" and "Reply to Fr. Murray"; Ottaviani, "Church and State: Some Present Problems in the Light of the Teaching of Pope Pius XII"; and Shea, "Catholic Doctrine and 'The Religion of the State.'"

3. See Chapter 3 above for a more complete consideration of this dispute between Murray and his contemporaries. See also Chapter 2, n. 20 for a possible explanation of Murray's omission of *Longinqua* from the "Leonine *corpus*" from which he garnered Leo's statement of the principles of social dualism.

4. Murray, "Leo XIII and Pius XII: Government and the Order of Religion," Galley 17, n. 9; Galley 26.

5. See John Paul II, *Centesimus Annus* (1991), no. 47, for a recent statement of the Church's recognition of the fundamental rights and freedoms which adhere to all human persons.

6. Murray, "Dr. Morrison and the First Amendment," *America* 78 (6 March 1948): 629.

7. This criticism of Murray's understanding of the philosophical bases of the American Founding has also recently been advanced in Michael J. Schuck, "John Courtney Murray's Problematic Interpretations of Leo XIII and the American Founders," *The Thomist* 55 (October 1991): 606-608, 610-612, and in J. Brian Benestad, "Catholicism and American Public Philosophy," *The Review of Politics* 53 (Fall 1991): 704-705.

8. *WHTT*, Chapter 13, "The Doctrine Lives," 303, 305.

9. Ibid., 304-305.

10. Ibid., 306.

11. Ibid., 307, 309.

12. Ibid., 313.

13. I refer here to Thomas Jefferson, author of the Declaration of Independence, and James Madison, principal architect of the U.S. Constitution and its Bill of Rights. The choice of these two great Virginia statesmen is meant neither to lionize these figures nor to denigrate the contributions of others. I refer exclusively to Jefferson and Madison simply because Murray himself endowed their political thought with a prominent place in his own interpretation of the philosophical bases of the American Founding.

14. Thomas Jefferson, "Declaration of Independence," July 4, 1776, in Merrill D. Peterson, ed. *The Portable Thomas Jefferson* (New York: The Viking Press, Inc., 1975), 235.

15. James Madison, *Federalist* 52 in William T. Hutchinson, William M.E. Rachal, *et al.*, ed., *The Papers of James Madison*, XV vols. (Chicago,IL: The University of Chicago Press and Charlottesville, VA: University Press of Virginia, 1962-1985), X, 521; "Spirit of Governments," *National Gazette*, February 18, 1792 in *Papers*, XIV, 234; and *Federalist* 10 in *Papers*, X, 265.

16. Madison, "Helvidius" Number 3 in *Papers*, XV, 98; and *Federalist* 57 in *Papers*, X, 523.

Appendix A

1. E.A. Goerner, *Peter and Caesar: The Catholic Church and Political Authority* (New York: Herder and Herder, 1965), 187, 188. Goerner added that "since the natural law tradition to which Murray adhered is rooted in Aristotle, it might not be foolish to note that of the two major works that contain his natural right teaching, one of them, the *Politics*, is almost wholly concerned with a theory of regimes." (Ibid., 188, n. 38.)

2. Ibid., 188-189.

3. John A. Rohr, "John Courtney Murray's Theology of Our Founding Fathers' 'Faith': Freedom" in Francis A. Eigo, ed., *Christian Spirituality in the United States: Independence and Interdependence* (Villanova, PA: The Villanova University Press, 1978), 22.

4. Murray, "The Problem of State Religion," 163.

5. Murray, "The Problem of Religious Freedom," 98.

6. Rohr, *op. cit.*, 23.

7. Charles E. Curran, *American Catholic Social Ethics: Twentieth Century Approaches* (Notre Dame, IN: University of Notre Dame Press, 1982), 223.

8. Ibid., 224. The only "contemporary theologian" to whom Curran explicitly refers in this assessment of Murray's work is Gustavo Gutierrez who is perhaps the most renowned liberation theologian, but whose works do not

necessarily represent the "mainstream" of Catholic theology, if such a "mainstream" exists at all. Curran might have provided further evidence to support this generalization.

9. Ibid., 224-225.

10. Ibid., 225-226.

11. Ibid., 230.

12. The objection that Murray's interpretation of the teaching of Leo XIII distorts the meaning intended by its author is also raised by Schuck in *op. cit.*, 602-606.

13. Ibid., 232.

14. This term was originally coined by Martin Marty in "Two Kinds of Civil Religion," in Russell E. Richey and David G. Jones, eds., *American Civil Religion* (New York: Harper and Row, 1974), 148. "Public theology" is a term which "refers to a self-consciously religious effort to form and mold . . . culture and politics so that they conform more fully with God's plan of salvation." (McElroy, *op. cit.*, 4.)

15. John A. Coleman, "A Possible Role for Biblical Religion in Public Life," in David Hollenbach, ed., "Theology and Philosophy in Public: A Symposium on John Courtney Murray's Unfinished Agenda," *TS* 40 (December 1979): 701-702, 705.

16. Ibid., 705. For Murray's appeal to the classical republican tradition as a source of public virtue see *WHTT*, 22, 46-47.

17. Ibid., 705-706.

18. Ibid., 706.

19. Robin W. Lovin, "Resources for a Public Theology," in Hollenbach, ed., "Theology and Philosophy in Public," 709-710.

20. One of the most helpful studies of the religious and philosophical bases of the First Amendment's guarantee of religious liberty is William Lee Miller's *The First Liberty: Religion and the American Republic* (New York: Paragon House Publishers, 1985). Miller describes the influence of both Deist and Protestant thinkers on the American understanding of religious liberty. He even goes so far as to claim that "the radical wing of the Protestant Reformation and of Puritanism . . . had more to do . . . with the shaping of the American tradition of religious liberty than did the rational Enlightenment." He concedes in his conclusion, however, that it is ironic that while the American understanding of the idea of religious liberty may indeed have "such metaphysical underpinnings, . . . any official, closed, final statement of them violates them." (153, 352.)

21. Hollenbach, "Public Theology in America: Some Questions for Catholicism After John Courtney Murray," *TS* 37 (June, 1976), 299.

22. Hollenbach, "Editor's Conclusion: A Fundamental Political Theology," in Hollenbach, ed., "Theology and Philosophy in Public," 714-715.

23. Ibid., 715.

24. McElroy, *op. cit.*, 148, 150.

25. Ibid., 154.

26. Hooper, *op. cit.*, 220.

27. See Bernard J.F. Lonergan, *Insight: A Study of Human Understanding* (New York: Longmans, Green and Co., Ltd., 1957); *Method in Theology* (New York: Herder and Herder, 1972).

28. Hooper, *op. cit.*, 223.

29. Ibid., 224.

30. Ibid., 224-225.

31. James T. Johnson, review of Thomas Shannon, ed., *War or Peace: The Search for New Answers*, in *Worldview* 24, no. 1 (January 1981): 21.

32. J. Bryan Hehir, "The Perennial Need for Philosophical Discourse," in Hollenbach, ed., "Theology and Philosophy in Public," 710-713. Emphasis added.

33. Ibid., 713.

34. Hehir, "Vatican II and the Signs of the Times: Catholic Teaching on Church, State, and Society," in Leslie Griffin, ed., *Religion and Politics in the American Milieu* (Notre Dame, IN: The Review of Politics, 1989), 71.

35. Richard J. Neuhaus, *The Naked Public Square: Religion and Democracy in America* (Grand Rapids, MI: William B. Erdmanns Publishing Co., 1984), 27.

36. Hehir, "Vatican II and the Signs of the Times," 72. Murray's analysis, to which Hehir refers, is that which he included in *WHTT*, Chapter 7, "Should There Be a Law?"

37. Ibid., 74.

38. Ibid., 76-77.

39. George Weigel, *Tranquilitas Ordinis: The Present Failure and Future Promise of American Catholic Thought on War and Peace* (New York: Oxford University Press, 1987), 322-324.

40. In fairness to Father Hehir, however, it must be noted that he has never claimed, nor desired, an exclusive role in carrying on Murray's legacy.

He has also demonstrated that the problems of communism and nuclear weapons have assumed very different characteristics in the years following Murray's death; they do not admit a simple application of Murray's policy prescriptions which might have been valid during the height of the Cold War. As to Weigel's charge that Hehir does not "celebrate America" as Murray did, I make no attempt to assess Hehir's patriotism but rather point to the significant differences in the nature of his and Murray's political-theological projects.

41. Weigel, *Catholicism and the Renewal of American Democracy* (New York: Paulist Press, 1989), 84-85.

42. Ibid., 87-88.

43. Ibid., 91.

44. Ibid., 95.

45. See Hooper, review of *Catholicism and the Renewal of American Democracy* in *America* 161 (19 August 1989): 88-90.

46. See Hollenbach, "War and Peace in American Catholic Thought: A Heritage Abandoned?" *TS* 48 (December, 1987): 711-726.

Appendix B

1. Reinhold Niebuhr, "Augustine's Political Realism," in *The Essential Reinhold Niebuhr: Selected Essays and Addresses*, ed. Robert McAfee Brown (New Haven, CT: Yale University Press, 1986), 125, 132-133.

2. Niebuhr, *Moral Man and Immoral Society* (New York: Charles Scribner's Sons, 1932), 29-30.

3. Niebuhr, *The Children of Light and the Children of Darkness* (New York: Charles Scribner's Sons, 1944), 10.

4. Niebuhr, *The Nature and Destiny of Man*, vol. I (New York: Charles Scribner's Sons, 1943), 16-17.

5. Niebuhr, *Moral Man*, 82.

Selected Bibliography

Works by Murray (arranged chronologically)

Murray, John Courtney, S.J. "Current Theology: Freedom of Religion." *Theological Studies (TS)* 6 (March 1945): 85-113.

----------. "Freedom of Religion I: The Ethical Problem." *TS* 6 (June 1945): 229-286.

----------. "How Liberal is Liberalism?" *America* 75 (6 April 1946): 6-7.

----------. "Separation of Church and State." *America* 76 (7 December 1946): 261-263.

----------. "Separation of Church and State: True and False Concepts." *America* 76 (15 February 1947): 541-545.

----------. "The Court Upholds Religious Freedom." *America* 76 (8 March 1947): 628-630.

----------. "Religious Liberty: The Concern of All." *America* 77 (7 February 1948): 513-516.

----------. "Dr. Morrison and the First Amendment." *America* 78 (6 March 1948): 627-629; (20 March 20 1948): 683-686.

----------. "Governmental Repression of Heresy." *Proceedings* of the Third Annual Convention of the Catholic Theological Society of America (1948): 26-98.

----------. "St. Robert Bellarmine on the Indirect Power." *TS* 9 (December 1948): 491-535.

----------. "Reversing the Secularist Drift." *Thought* 24 (March 1949): 36-46.

----------. "Contemporary Orientations of Catholic Thought on Church and State in the Light of History." *TS* 10 (June 1949): 177-234.

----------. "Current Theology: On Religious Freedom." *TS* 10 (September 1949): 409-432.

----------. "The Problem of State Religion." *TS* 12 (June 1951): 155-78.

----------. "For the Freedom and Transcendence of the Church." *The American Ecclesiastical Review (AER)* 126 (January 1952): 28-48.

----------. "The Church and Totalitarian Democracy." *TS* 13 (December 1952): 525-563.

----------. "Leo XIII on Church and State: The General Structure of the Controversy." *TS* 14 (March 1953): 1-30.

----------. "Leo XIII: Separation of Church and State." *TS* 14 (June 1953): 145-214.

----------. "Leo XIII: Two Concepts of Government." *TS* 14 (December 1953): 551-563.

----------. "Leo XIII: Two Concepts of Government: Government and the Order of Culture." *TS* 15 (March 1954): 1-33.

----------. "On the Structure of the Church-State Problem." In *The Catholic Church in World Affairs*, ed. Waldemar Gurian and M.A. Fitzimmons, 11-32. Notre Dame, IN: University of Notre Dame Press, 1954.

----------. "Leo XIII and Pius XII: Government and the Order of Religion." (1955) John Courtney Murray Papers (Archives of Woodstock College, Georgetown University, Washington, DC), file 536.

----------. "Law or Prepossessions?" In *Essays in Constitutional Law*, ed. Robert G. McCloskey, 316-347. New York: Alfred A. Knopf, Inc., 1957.

----------. "Church and State: The Structure of the Argument." (1958) Murray Papers, file 490.

----------. *"Unica Status Religio."* (1959) Murray Papers, file 561.

----------. *We Hold These Truths: Catholic Reflections on the American Proposition.* New York: Sheed & Ward, 1960.

----------. "The Return to Tribalism." *The Catholic Mind* 60 (January 1962): 5-12.

----------. "On Religious Liberty." *America* 109 (30 November 1963): 704-706.

----------. *The Problem of Religious Freedom*, Woodstock Papers, Number 7. Westminster, MD: The Newman Press, 1965.

----------. "This Matter of Religious Freedom." *America* 112 (9 January 1965): 40-43.

----------. "Religious Freedom." In *Freedom and Man,* ed. John Courtney Murray, 131-140. New York: P.J. Kenedy, 1965.

----------. "Religious Freedom." In *The Documents of Vatican II,* ed. Walter M. Abbott and Joseph Gallagher, Introduction, 673-674; Text with Commentary, 674-698. New York: America Press, 1966.

----------. "The Vatican Declaration on Religious Freedom: An Aspect of Its Significance." In *The University in the American Experience,* 1-10. New York: Fordham University Press, 1966.

----------. "The Declaration on Religious Liberty: Its Deeper Significance." *America* 114 (23 April 1966): 592-593.

----------. "The Declaration on Religious Freedom: A Moment in Its Legislative History." In *Religious Liberty: An End and a Beginning,* ed. John Courtney Murray, 15-42. New York: Macmillan and Co., 1966).

----------. "The Declaration on Religious Freedom." In *Vatican II: An Interfaith Appraisal,* ed. John H. Miller, Article, 565-576; Discussion, 577-585. Notre Dame, IN: Association Press, 1966.

----------. "The Issue of Church and State at Vatican II." *TS* 27 (December 1966): 580-606.

Secondary Sources

Abraham, Henry J. *Freedom and the Court: Civil Rights and Liberties in the United States,* 5th ed. New York: Oxford University Press, 1988.

Benestad, J. Brian. "Catholicism and American Public Philosophy." *The Review of Politics* 53 (Fall 1991): 691-711.

Benevot, Maurice. "Thesis and Hypothesis." *TS* 15 (September 1954): 440-446.

Burghart, Walter J. "Who Chilled the Beaujolais?" *America* 153 (30 November 1985): 360-363.

Canavan, Francis J. "Murray on Vatican II's Declaration on Religious Freedom." *Communio* 9 (Winter 1982): 404-405.

Carlyle, Robert W. and A.J. Carlyle. *A History of Medieval Political Theory in the West,* 6 vols. New York: Barnes & Noble, Inc., 1903-1936.

Cogley, John, ed. Religion in America: Original Essays on Religion in a Free Society. New York: The World Publishing Co., 1958.

Coleman, John A. "Vision and Praxis in American Theology: Orestes Brownson, John A. Ryan, and John Courtney Murray." *TS* 37 (March 1976): 3-40.

Connell, Francis J. "Pope Leo XIII's Message to America." *AER* 109 (October 1943): 249-256.

----------. "Reply to Fr. Murray." *AER* 126 (January 1952):49-59.

----------. "The Theory of the 'Lay State.'" *AER* 125 (July 1951): 7-18.

Curran, Charles E. *American Catholic Social Ethics: Twentieth Century Approaches.* Notre Dame, IN: University of Notre Dame Press, 1982.

----------. *Catholic Moral Theology in Dialogue.* Notre Dame, IN: University of Notre Dame Press, 1973.

Eigo, Francis A., ed. *Christian Spirituality in the United States: Independence and Interdependence.* Villanova, PA: The Villanova University Press, 1978.

Fenton, Joseph C. "The Catholic Church and Freedom of Religion." *AER* 115 (October 1946): 286-301.

----------. "The Theology of the Church and the State." *Proceedings* of the Second Annual Meeting of the Catholic Theological Society of America. (1947): 15-46.

----------. "The Status of a Controversy." *AER* 124 (June 1951): 451-458.

----------. "Principles Underlying Traditional Church-State Doctrine." *AER* 126 (June 1952): 452-462.

----------. "The Teachings of *Ci riesce.*" *AER* 130 (February 1954): 114-123.

----------. "Toleration and the Church-State Controversy." *AER* 130 (May 1954): 330-343.

Fogarty, Gerald P. *The Vatican and the American Hierarchy from 1870 to 1965.* Wilmington, DE: Michael Glazier, Inc., 1985.

Goerner, E.A. *Peter and Caesar: The Catholic Church and Political Authority.* New York: Herder and Herder, 1965.

Griffin, Leslie, ed. *Religion and Politics in the American Milieu.* The Review of Politics, 1989.

Gurian, Waldemar and M.A. Fitzsimons, eds. *The Catholic Church in World Affairs.* Notre Dame, IN: University of Notre Dame Press, 1954.

Gustafson, James M. *Christian Ethics and the Community.* Philadelphia, PA: United Church Press, 1971.

Hehir, J. Bryan. "The Unfinished Agenda." *America* 153 (30 November 1985): 386-387, 392.

Higgins, George G. "Some Personal Recollections." *America* 153 (November 30, 1985): 380-386.

Hollenbach, David. "The Growing End of an Argument." *America* 153 (November 30, 1985): 363-366.

----------. "Public Theology in America: Some Questions for Catholicism After John Courtney Murray." *TS* 37 (June 1976): 290-303.

----------., ed. "Theology and Philosophy in Public: A Symposium on John Courtney Murray's Unfinished Agenda." *TS* 40 (December 1979): 700-715.

----------. "War and Peace in American Catholic Thought: A Heritage Abandoned?" *TS* 48 (December 1987): 711-726.

Hooper, J. Leon. "Catholicism and the Renewal of American Democracy." *America* 161 (19 August 1989): 88-90.

----------. *The Ethics of Discourse: The Social Philosophy of John Courtney Murray.* Washington, DC: Georgetown University Press, 1986.

Hughes, Philip. *A Popular History of the Catholic Church.* New York: MacMillan Publishing Co., Inc., 1947.

Hunt, George W. "Of Many Things." *America* 153 (30 November 1985): 356.

Lawler, Peter Augustine. "Natural Law and the American Regime: Murray's *We Hold These Truths.*" *Communio* 9 (Winter 1982): 368-388.

Leclercq, J. *Jean de Paris et l'ecclesiologie du XIIIe siecle.* Paris, 1942.

Lonergan, Bernard J.F. *Insight: A Study of Human Understanding.* New York: Philosophical Library, 1957.

----------. *Method in Theology.* New York: Herder and Herder, 1972.

Love, Thomas T. *John Courtney Murray: Contemporary Church-State Theory.* Garden City, NY: Doubleday and Company, Inc., 1965.

MacIver, R.M., ed. *Great Expressions of Human Rights: A Series of Addresses and Discussions.* New York: Harper and Brothers, 1950.

McBrien, Richard P. *Caesar's Coin: Religion and Politics in America.* New York: MacMillan Publishing Co., 1987.

McCloskey, Robert G., ed. *Essays in Constitutional Law.* New York: Alfred A. Knopf, Inc., 1957.

McElroy, Robert W. *The Search for an American Public Theology: The Contribution of John Courtney Murray.* New York: Paulist Press, 1989.

McEvoy, Raymond O. "John Courtney Murray's Thought on Religious Liberty in its Final Phase." S.T.D. diss. Pontifical Lateran University, 1973.

McManus, William E. "Memories of Murray." *America* 153 (30 November 1985): 366-368.

Miller, William E. *The First Liberty: Religion and the American Republic.* New York: Paragon House Publishers, 1985.

Mooney, Christopher F. *Public Virtue: Law and the Social Character of Religion.* Notre Dame, IN: University of Notre Dame Press, 1986.

Neuhaus, Richard John. *The Naked Public Square.* Grand Rapids, MI: William B. Erdmanns Publishing Co., 1984.

Oaks, Dallin H., ed. *The Wall Between Church and State.* Chicago, IL: University of Chicago Press, 1963.

Ottaviani, Alfredo Cardinal. "Church and State: Some Present Problems in the Light of the Teaching of Pope Pius XII." *AER* 128 (May 1953): 321-334.

----------. *Institutiones iuris publici ecclesiastici*, 2 vols. Rome: Typis Polyglottis Vaticanis, 1947-1948.

Pelotte, Donald E. *John Courtney Murray: Theologian in Conflict.* New York: Paulist Press, 1975.

Pius XII. *"Ci Riesce*: A Discourse to the National Convention of Italian Catholic Jurists: Official Vatican Press Office English Translation." *AER* 130 (February 1954): 129-138.

Rohr, John A. "John Courtney Murray and the Pastoral Letters." *America* 153 (30 November 1985): 373-379.

Schuck, Michael J. "John Courtney Murray's Problematic Interpretations of Leo XIII and the American Founders." *The Thomist* 55 (October 1991): 595-612.

Shannon, Thomas A., ed. *War or Peace? The Search for New Answers.* Maryknoll, NY: Orbis Books, 1980.

Shea, George W. "Catholic Doctrine and 'The Religion of the State.'" *AER* 123 (September 1950): 161-174.

Sigmund, Paul E., ed. *St. Thomas Aquinas on Politics and Ethics.* New York: W.W. Norton & Co., 1988.

Thompson, Kenneth W. *Masters of International Thought: Major Twentieth Century Theorists and the World Crisis.* Baton Rouge, LA: Louisiana State University Press, 1980.

Weigel, George. *Catholicism and the Renewal of American Democracy.* New York: Paulist Press, 1989.

----------. *Tranquilitas Ordinis: The Present Failure and Future Promise of American Catholic Thought on War and Peace.* New York: Oxford University Press, 1987.

Whelan, Charles M. "The Enduring Problems of Religious Liberty." *America* 153 (30 November 1985): 368-372.

Index

186